ONE
AFTERNOON
AT MEZZEGRA

ONE AFTERNOON AT MEZZEGRA

Peter Whittle

PRENTICE-HALL, INC., ENGLEWOOD CLIFFS, N. J.

To Freddie Sutton,
with heartfelt gratitude

ACKNOWLEDGEMENTS

When one spends eighteen months of one's life wrestling with the problems involved with a book such as this, there are many reasons to thank many people. But there are really too many to enumerate individually—they would fill a small book by themselves.

But I should like to express particular thanks to the following: Nicholas Thompson, to whom I turned often for Scotch and encouragement and who was never lacking in either.

My wife, who rarely complained during all those months and all those thousands of miles around Europe, who cared for and coddled not only myself and our small daughter while travelling through nine countries, but who managed, with impeccable timing, to present us with a son on the day the manuscript was finished.

To the others—Miss Marjorie Bolton in London; Erwin Chlanda in Vienna; Les Childe in Rome; Eric Whittle in Paris; Mrs. Marion Bilgeri in Domaso; Miss Lise Sinclair and the many I met and received help from—go my sincere thanks.

*A section of illustrations appears
between pages
62-63*

INTRODUCTION

The killing of Benito Mussolini and the public orgy in the Piazzale Loreto, Milan, which followed, remains one of the most gruesome episodes of World War Two. It was an act reminiscent of the bloodsports of Ancient Rome.

That Mussolini deserved no better fate, that his execution was a fortuitous means of avoiding the ritual killing which would surely have followed a War Crimes trial, is a viable viewpoint. Yet the event remains what it surely was—a brutal and bloody act of mob vengeance.

The tragedy of Sunday, April 29, 1945, when thousands of Milanese were caught up in the horror of the Piazzale Loreto has been the subject of many books but what has always seemed to me to be far more intriguing is the sequence of events which led up to that moment. And in this book, I have attempted to retrace those events through the eyes, minds and feelings of the people who took part in them and who survived to tell of them.

Mussolini was doomed from the moment he decided to leave Milan on April 25, 1945. From that instant he was a man on the run with nowhere to go. At the age of sixty-one, with all his former power and glory in tatters, he seems to have lacked the will to escape a fate which he must have known was about to overtake him.

The snap judgement of history labels Mussolini as a buffoon, an adventurer in the world of power politics, a hesitant gambler in a game where the stakes were always too high. Yet it cannot be denied that Mussolini ruled Italy for twenty-one years, and gave his country a span of political continuity longer than that enjoyed by any European country between the wars. But like too many others he was hunted and finally destroyed in his own country and by his own countrymen. Mussolini may have been a pathetic figure in life, but it is in his death that the real pathos lies.

The other outstanding element in the story—and perhaps the only sympathetic element—is the fidelity of the woman who chose to remain with Mussolini to the very end and who died ignominiously with him at the roadside in Mezzegra. Of all who followed Mussolini in the last hours, Clara Petacci was probably the only one who went gladly and willingly, having rejected a clear and safe alternative.

In order to piece together the events of the last five days in the lives of those two doomed people I set out to find as many witnesses as possible. Many had told their stories briefly and had since vanished. Some had died. Some had spoken once and refused to speak again. Some refused to say a word. Some were untraceable. But fortunately I found some who were ready and able to dig deeply into their memories.

I am particularly grateful to Herr Fritz Birzer, now the proprietor of a flourishing wood-panelling factory in Munich. As the German officer detailed to guard Mussolini throughout the flight from Milan, Herr Birzer was one of the key witnesses and threw much light on the personality of Mussolini as well as on his own motives and actions during those days.

Another valuable German source was Herr Wilhelm Hurtmanns. A former Wehrmacht propaganda officer, he was in Milan during Mussolini's preparations for the journey to Lake Como. He went on the fateful journey, and returned to Milan in time to witness the grim scenes in the Piazzale Loreto. As a professional observer, Herr Hurtmanns was particularly useful and I am indebted to him for allowing me access to an unpublished book on those events, which he wrote in 1947 after returning to Germany from Milan. This book yielded much material now unavailable to researchers since it includes interviews with people who have since died.

The most important of the Italian sources was Signor Pier Bellini delle Stelle. Now a Public Relations officer with the Italian state petrocarbon combine ENI, Signor Bellini was, in 1945, the commander of the partisan group which captured Mussolini. Signor Bellini allowed me to interview him at length, with particular regard to the conversations he himself had with Mussolini and Clara Petacci.

Much of the material which has enabled me to paint an accurate picture of Clara Petacci was obtained from Herr Franz Spögler. At the hotel he now owns high in the Italian Tyrol, he was kind enough to give me his account of the nature and personality of Clara Petacci—impressions he formed during many months as her closest protector.

Many other people gave their time and advice, filling in pieces of the whole story, and helping to provide essential detail to the general structure. To all these I am most grateful.

Without them, I could not have attempted to give an accurate picture of the five days which span the period of the narrative. With their help, I have managed to reconstruct a story that will, perhaps, make some contribution to historical documentation.

In as many cases as possible, I have cross-checked each individual story before weaving it into the whole and have rejected a great deal of lively hearsay. The conversations I have quoted, for example, are only those which I was able to re-create with the help of living witnesses.

The one major disappointment was the failure of all my attempts to interview Signor Walter Audisio, the man who actually shot Mussolini and Petacci, and who is now a member of the Italian parliament. However, Signor Audisio has written three separate accounts of his experiences and although they differ in detail, there is an overall consistency.

I have of course, read most of the books dealing with the life of Mussolini, and I would like to acknowledge my debt to their authors for some valuable background material.

I have made no attempt in this book to strike an attitude—

either moral or political—on the events with which I have dealt. I have merely recorded and reconstructed many episodes and facts in the belief that they will indicate not only what things men did during these days, but also why they did them.

Dunsfold, February 1969

I

The wet streets of the city were eerily quiet after the noise of the day. The only perceptible movement was the silent shift of the rain clouds that scudded low over the roofs: there was almost no lighting so that every street was a fearsome canyon, a foreboding valley of sightless windows, shutters and locked doors.

Earlier there had been gunshots, bursts of automatic weapon fire, the occasional dull thump of distant artillery, but now there was only a brooding silence. Like some destructive drunk, collapsed and paralytic after a mindless orgy, the city of Milan was sleeping. Soon there was to be one final fling of wanton savagery but at this moment, at three o'clock in the morning of April 29, 1945, the city was still.

Across the ravaged face of Europe the closing battles of the Second World War were being fought.

The armies of East and West had finally touched hands three days before when advance patrols of General Hodges' US First Army had met those of the Soviet First Ukrainian Army on the River Elbe and Russians and Americans had hugged each other in the effusive glow of victory.

The Nazi Thousand-Year Third Reich lay in ruins only twelve years after its birth and, at the heart of it, Adolf Hitler was cornered in his bunker forty feet beneath the burning rubble of Berlin as Russian infantry pushed relentlessly towards him.

In Italy, the Allied victory was almost complete. Later this very day, the beaten German commanders were to sign the unconditional surrender of their forces, while Italy itself was torn by civil war.

Milan, previously by-passed in the American drive northward, had been seized by partisans and for four days they had been wreaking bloody vengeance on their former Fascist masters. For ordinary Milanese, it was a nervous, uneasy time: a time to ask no questions; to observe but say nothing; a time to wait and see.

Giuseppe Marchi stirred in his bed and opened his eyes. For a moment, he listened to the silence in his little three-roomed apartment on the Viale Padova in the north-west of the city. His wife, Maria, breathed steadily, deep asleep in the bed next to him. For a moment he could not identify the unfamiliar noise that had woken him, but then he heard it again. It was the low drone of a heavy motor. It drew closer, it was almost certainly approaching along Viale Padova and at last Marchi could see the soft glow of headlights seeping through the slats of the window shutters.

Quietly, he eased himself out of bed and tip-toed to the window. Through the crack between the shutters, he caught a glimpse of a large covered lorry moving slowly along the street below. The headlights, though shaded, still picked out the tramlines and the big wet cobblestones of the road. He watched the tail lights draw away and finally disappear into the lake of blackness that was the Piazzale Loreto, a vast open square where five main roads met.

As the sound of the motor diminished he crept back to bed, vaguely curious. In the ordinary way, the passing of a truck in the night would have meant nothing, but in late April 1945, nothing was ordinary in Milan.

After weeks of uncertainty, it was now clear that it was the end of the war, the end of occupation by the Germans to whom Italy had been a half-hearted ally, the end of Mussolini's Fascism. Everything seemed to have collapsed with bewildering suddenness.

Mussolini—Il Duce—who had gathered the last remnants of his former glory around him in the city which had been the mainspring of his power nearly a quarter of a century before, had finally departed. The long-awaited uprising of armed partisans in the city had begun and in its wake there had been an orgy of bloodshed and indiscriminate shooting. As old enemies were killed, new enemies took their places. Already an estimated five thousand people had died.

The Germans had barely bothered to defend the city. Those who garrisoned the key strongpoints had pulled out, drawn into the swelling flood of retreat from the broken front line.

A general strike added to the confusion. The shops were shut, trams no longer ran and the air was filled with rumour; conflicting orders of the day came from conflicting authorities. In this ambience of tension and fear the passing of a truck in the middle of the night was something to be reckoned with.

Giuseppe Marchi drifted back to sleep, unaware that he had witnessed the return to Milan of Benito Mussolini.

Il Duce was back—back to the city from which he had begun his last journey just five days before. He had left Milan nursing a pathetic hope of salvation. Trailing behind him had been the last loyal adherents of a government with no power to govern—men who followed him to the end simply because they had nowhere else to go, nor any hope.

Through twenty-three years of heady triumph and slow decline, they had stood with him, cheering as millions had cheered when the spellbinding oratory had flowed from confidence backed by the might of the Rome–Berlin Axis. And, when the oratory had ceased and the cheering had become only a mocking echo of the past, this band of loyalists remained with him—doomed men, about to die.

Now, along with their leader, their bullet-riddled corpses lay in hideous ignominy inside that blood-stained lorry which had crept in the night along Viale Padova and stopped in the Piazzale Loreto. The macabre load comprised the corpses of seventeen men and one woman—Mussolini's tragically faithful mistress, Clara Petacci. She had paid the penalty of her fidelity to Mussolini—with six shots in her beautiful body fired from an automatic rifle.

When the lorry had come to a stop, ten weary men jumped to the pavement alongside a bomb-damaged petrol station and began to unload their grisly cargo. They worked slowly, for they had not slept in forty-eight hours and had witnessed scenes which would keep them awake for many more nights. One by one, they heaved the corpses to the ground until all eighteen lay in grotesque confusion on the stones. Then the lorry was driven away and the remaining eight men, propping their guns against the girders of the filling station, sat down to rest.

Some smoked, others slept, but they remained largely silent, contemplating the obscene heap lying in front of them.

Benito Mussolini, his head cradled perchance on the arm of his mistress, stared sightless into the night sky.

A thousand miles away in Berlin, 300 feet below the thunder of Russian artillery, Mussolini's evil partner Adolf Hitler leaned on the arm of *his* mistress Eva Braun. They were being married. It was nine days after Hitler's fifty-sixth birthday and a little less than thirty-six hours before his death. The once mighty Nazi Reich was dissolving in flames, lighting its creator to ignominious death. Twelve million people had died and others were still dying as a result of his crazed bid for power. Benito Mussolini was just one of the casualties.

Was it coincidence that the two tyrants who hoped jointly to conquer Europe would, within a few days of each other, die as obscurely as the millions they had slaughtered in the years of their triumph?

As the city of Milan began to wake on the morning of April 29th, 1945, the rumour was rife that Mussolini was dead. It was being said that his body was actually lying in the square renamed by the Resistance as the Square of the Fifteen Martyrs in memory of fifteen Italians whom the Germans had murdered (on

August 13, 1944) as a reprisal for German soldiers killed by the partisans.

Soon, people began to move from all parts of the city—since rumour has powerful wings—towards the square, and by eight o'clock there was a huge crowd, growing bigger by the minute, surrounding the pile of corpses beside the disused petrol station.

An hour later, the eight weary partisans guarding the bodies were overwhelmed and completely lost control of the situation. Mass hysteria seized the onlookers and what was at first a horrified and awed crowd turned suddenly into a berserk howling mob.

They spat and kicked at the bodies and gave vent to all the frustration of a bewildered people. A woman pushed her way to the front of the crowd and suddenly produced a loaded gun. She pumped five shots into the body of the man her compatriots had so recently cheered in the streets. She screamed that the five shots were repayment for the death of five sons lost in Mussolini's war, those around her applauded her fury and waded in again to kick and spit and revile. They laughed at the sickeningly contorted features of their Duce and yelled sexual obscenities at the half-clothed body of his mistress.

Two of the partisans fired shots in the air but to no avail. Some others tried to rig up a water hose to drive away the hysterical crowd which pressed so hard around the petrol station that some were actually standing on the corpses—but the hose might well have been pumping champagne for all it did to lessen the intoxication of the moment.

Yuone Fancelli was one of those in the crowd. He had been wakened from an exhausted sleep by the sound of gunshots and had come running from his bed in a house on Viale Padova. A serviceman in the crack Italian marine unit, the Decima MAS, he had left Milan with Mussolini four days before. Then, still moved by the presence of Mussolini, he had willingly joined the dwindling band of men and women who accompanied him on his last

17

journey. Now the sight of that ravaged corpse made only one impression on him. He felt physically ill.

By one o'clock in the afternoon, Piazzale Loreto was full. From all over Milan, people pressed towards the place but could now get no nearer than the streets leading into it. It was then that one of the mob decided to stage the revolting finale to the hideous performance. A big muscular man, wearing a light-coloured shirt smeared with congealed blood, he trampled on the bodies and turned to the crowd from the top of his bloody platform.

"Which one do you want to see?" he roared. In answer to the shouts from a thousand throats, he bent and lifted Mussolini above his head. Mussolini's legs waved gently in the air, the left one still wearing a jackboot. His head flopped backwards and his eyes remained open. The crowd roared for more.

Petacci was next. Her thighs were caked with blood, but in death her bruised and muddied face remained curiously serene, almost smiling, remote from the violence.

And still the crowd howled for more. Amid the confusion, someone produced a length of rope. Mussolini's ankles were tied and the other end of the rope thrown over the horizontal girder running the length of the filling station canopy. Slowly, the corpse was hoisted up and hung there, upside-down, arms extended like an inverted scarecrow.

Petacci was strung up next to him, but in a moment of dreadful propriety, a woman stepped forward and tucked Petacci's skirt between her legs to hide her nakedness, and tied it with a piece of rag.

Then two more corpses were strung up and each time the crowd cheered. Some clambered on to the roof of the petrol station and waved in triumph. Then someone pinned pieces of cardboard to the corpses with names scrawled in paint. Many of the crowd had been to early morning Mass and most wore their best clothes, a few with partisan armbands and carrying rifles.

Wilhelm Hurtmanns began taking photographs with a 35 mm. Leica camera—the same Leica he had carried with him throughout the German campaigns in the Balkans, Greece, Crete, North Africa and Italy. Some of the people nearest to the hanging bodies noticed Hurtmanns and smilingly posed before his camera as they would for a holiday snapshot.

The news of Mussolini's death spread quickly across the world. With Hitler still enigmatically sealed in the depths of the bunker in Berlin, the tangible downfall of one of the great dictators symbolised the end of an era. For just a few more hours Mussolini eclipsed Hitler as a figurehead of oppression. Just for a few hours, his were the headlines.

Donna Rachele Mussolini heard of her husband's death on the radio in the villa near Como where she had, a couple of days before, received the last message written by her husband. A German-language radio station in Switzerland repeated the news in hourly bulletins and it was from one of these broadcasts that the news came to Fritz Birzer as he trudged through a Swiss village on a road that led back towards Germany. Birzer, who had tried harder than anyone to save the life of Mussolini, now knew that he had failed—and he was filled with a kind of dread of the consequences.

Adolf Hitler heard the news of his comrade's death with apparent unemotion, and barely commented on it. He himself had long since resolved that he would not fall into enemy hands and the plans for his suicide and the disposal of his body had already been made and finalised. Even in death, Mussolini meant little to him.

Meanwhile, Mussolini's body swayed slowly on the rope. The one-time ruler of a nation, a dictator once more powerful than Hitler, the conquerer of Abyssinia, the oratorical spellbinder, dangled incongruously before his once devoted countrymen.

And then, almost suddenly, the crowd quietened. They began to talk in whispers as if half afraid of still being there. It seemed as if everyone realised that they had witnessed and been part of a terrible tragedy, an exhibition of mass hatred.

At about one o'clock in the afternoon, a detachment of partisans put an end to the ghastly spectacle. Forcing their way through the mass, they reached the filling station and cut down the suspended corpses. The crowd started to drift away. The bodies of Mussolini, Petacci and the others were taken to the mortuary in the city where they joined the endless stream of other corpses washed up on the tide of revenge which had swept across Italy at the collapse of Fascism.

2

Untersturmfuhrer-SS Fritz Birzer was nagged by an uneasy feeling as he stood staring out across the courtyard of the Milan Prefecture in the early afternoon of Wednesday, April 25, 1945. It was partly that he was hungry. He had not eaten since early morning and it would be a while yet before he could get food. Half his squad of Waffen-SS men were having a meal at the barracks of the Italian Fascist "Muti" police, twenty minutes away from the Prefecture by car.

Until they returned, Birzer would get by on cigarettes. Only then would he take his other eleven men to eat. It was just as they had taught him at the SS Leader School in Munich the year before—look after your men first, they had drummed into him. And Birzer had understood, probably better than his instructors. After all, until the end of 1943, he himself had been only an ordinary soldier serving on the Russian front near Smolensk.

Birzer was standing at the window of a ground-floor office which had once belonged to the Prefecture secretariat. He and his men had commandeered it when they arrived in the Prefecture with Mussolini nearly a week before. There had been desks in the office then, and typewriters and files and all the appearances of a normal, smoothly functioning government office. But that had been nearly a week ago. Since then, Birzer's Waffen-SS men had cleared out the desks and replaced them with mattresses. A gaggle of Italian secretaries had turned up for work the morning after, and Birzer smiled as he recalled the look on their faces when he had told them to go home and forget about work for a while. They had scarcely understood his halting Italian, overlaid with a Bavarian accent, but they had got the message. They knew, anyway, that everything had changed. Il Duce had arrived.

Even as he remembered, Birzer looked up at the first-floor window opposite him in the adjacent corner of the Prefecture and as his brown eyes studied the blank glass, that uneasy feeling returned to his stomach.

It wasn't only hunger; and it wasn't fear. He had lived with fear in Russia and that was different. It was more the lonely tension of a man in the dark in strange surroundings, waiting for something to happen. And the key to it all was on the other side of that first-floor window, where Mussolini had his quarters and his office. There, Il Duce received an endless flow of visitors. Ministers of the Fascist Republic, Army officers, leading local Fascists from Milan and the province of Lombardy and a host of other men and women whom Birzer neither knew nor particularly cared about. He knew and cared about only one thing—to carry out his orders, which were to watch over Mussolini, stay with him and protect him, at all costs.

Untersturmfuhrer Birzer had been given these orders seven days previously, when he and three other officers of the 2/2 SS Flak Abteilung had been warned that Mussolini was about to leave his heavily guarded headquarters on Lake Garda for a short visit to see Italian Republican Army troops in the front line on the River Po and to take stock of the precarious military situation. It was not known when Mussolini would leave, but each of the four Untersturmfuhrers who commanded the SS guard in rotation were briefed to leave at a moment's notice with their own platoon of seasoned combat soldiers. Whoever happened to be on duty when Il Duce elected to leave would be responsible for Mussolini's safety.

And Providence had chosen Birzer.

At first, he hadn't minded. A trip to the front would at least be a break from guard duty at Mussolini's compound, where the Duce was no more than a prisoner living inside barbed wire with all communications tapped. Birzer disliked the role of warder.

It had been at about three in the afternoon of April 18 when Birzer had been informed that Mussolini would leave Gargnano, where he had been set up with his puppet government by the Germans. Mussolini had been in a good mood. Dressed in the green-grey uniform of the Fascist Militia, with tasselled cap and jackboots, he said goodbye to his wife Donna Rachele at the Villa Feltrinelli, climbed into his Alfa-Romeo and swept through the barbed wire gate on his first journey in weeks. Behind him drove two carloads of plain-clothes security men belonging to the Sicherheitsdienst—the SD—whose job was to watch Mussolini and report his movements and actions to the Reich Sicherheit-hauptampt—security office—in Berlin. They were under the command of Kriminalinspektor Otto Kisnatt, a heavily-built forty-eight-year-old expert watchdog who had once done a similar surveillance on the ageing Reich President Hindenburg during the last days of his life.

Behind them came Fritz Birzer in a Volkswagen Kubelwagen—the German equivalent of a jeep—and a lorry load of Waffen-SS men armed with automatic weapons, heavy machine guns and an anti-tank gun. But the convoy did not head for the front line. There had been a last-moment change of plans. Mussolini had told his German masters that he intended going first to Milan, and so the line of vehicles drove through the dusk to Brescia, Bergamo and into Milan. They made the journey without incident and (probably because of the weather) without a sign of Allied aircraft.

They had arrived in the Prefecture in Milan at nine o'clock in the evening, and had remained there ever since.

Now, Birzer's sad, bony face reflected the gloom he felt. What was to have been a four-day tour had dragged on into nearly a week. What he had envisaged as an organised procession had become a chaotic mêlée. Where there should have been plans, orders and controlled movements to rely upon, there was now no plan, no orders, no control. Only confusion.

Birzer fished in the breast pocket of his grey tunic, pulled out a crumpled packet of cigarettes and lit one, still watchful. As always, the courtyard of the Prefecture resembled a children's playground. It seemed to him that nobody walked when they could run, nobody spoke when they could shout and certainly nobody stopped to tell Birzer what was going on. And, in truth, even if they had, Birzer would not have believed them. He did not like or trust the Italians. He could only feel that something was about to happen, something that would test to the limit the orders he had been given in the briefing room at Gargnano, shortly before he had set out.

"Mussolini must be guarded at all times," Haupsturmfuhrer Joost had ordered. "You must not let him out of your sight for a moment." And then he had added, almost as an afterthought. "Rather than surrender him to anyone, you will, in the last resort, turn your weapons on him. And shoot to kill."

For the next four days those orders—and the consequences if he failed to obey them—were to haunt him.

A few hundred metres away from the Prefecture, in the first-floor apartment at 3 Corso Littorio, Clara Petacci was also waiting. She had come to Milan the day after Mussolini, determined, as always, to be near her lover and protector.

At thirty-three, Petacci still retained the dark, carefully-groomed good looks which had attracted Mussolini thirteen years before. During those years, their affair had remained tempestuous, lusty, scandalous and constant. While Il Duce remained dutiful to his wife and proud and affectionate to the children she bore him, while his inordinate sexual appetite had many outlets, there was no one who could challenge Clara Petacci's influence over him.

The Germans had long realised that in order to keep a tight watch on Mussolini, it was necessary also to keep an eye on Clara and to carry out this task they assigned the good-looking Franz Spögler, a thirty-year-old SS Obersturmfuhrer. He took on the job in November 1943 and, faithful to his orders, had rarely strayed from Clara's presence in the intervening seventeen months. It was Spögler, now the friend of the entire Petacci family, who had attended the last family gathering on the night of April 19, when the Petaccis had begged Clara to accompany them on a flight to Spain—a flight largely organised by the sympathetic Spögler. The evening had been a melancholy one, for Clara had adamantly refused all the entreaties of her family and had declared with impressive sincerity that her place was in Italy. "Half my heart will go with you to Spain," she had said, "but the rest of me belongs to Il Duce. I must go wherever he goes."

This had ended the discussion and the remainder of the evening was spent in anguished farewells. But having turned down her last chance to escape from Italy, she was a frightened woman. Installed in the apartment on Corso Littorio, she became convinced she was being watched. The Fascist Black Brigade trooper patrolling the pavement opposite the apartment was, she imagined, a partisan in disguise. Spögler did his best to reassure her and sometimes succeeded. At such times Petacci became her old self, and engaged in a twitter of feminine activity. She altered the style of her long black hair, brushed the lashes of her big dark eyes, read romantic novels, played records of her favourite composer, Rossini, looked at herself in the mirror and frequently changed her dress. But it rarely lasted long, and on April 24, when Spögler last saw her, she was crying bitterly. Spögler, who had to go to Lake Garda to bring back some documents for Mussolini, promised he would not be away long. He took a list of the luggage she wanted brought to Milan and he tried to comfort her by saying she would be well looked after by his Italian counterpart, Lieutenant Michele di Domenico, who would remain in Milan with her.

But still she wept.

Otto Kisnatt was not by nature a man who worried unduly. An experienced officer of the Sicherheitdienst, he had risen to the rank of Kriminalinspektor through methodical devotion to his duty and orders. And since the beginning of 1945 he had carried out his orders concerning Benito Mussolini with unfailing efficiency. Every week, his reports went to Berlin—reports which soothed any fears of the Nazi hierarchy that Mussolini might make a new bid for real power. Kisnatt recorded Mussolini's every move, interpreted every word the Italian leader spoke to him, and presented a total picture of a figurehead, decked out with the trappings of power, but utterly powerless.

And while Fritz Birzer stood worrying in the Prefecture in Milan, Otto Kisnatt was equally perturbed. He had been directed to return to Garda with Spögler, and shortly before he left Milan, Kisnatt had spoken earnestly with the Duce, getting from him a promise that he would not budge from the city until he, Kisnatt, returned.

Borrowing a lorry from Birzer's Waffen-SS group, Kisnatt therefore departed late on Tuesday, April 24, his purpose to break up and destroy his office in Gargnano and bring files and equipment back to Milan. Travelling all night, he got to Gargnano early on the 25th and began his work. Throughout the day, he sorted through his files, burning everything but the most important ones. A squad of SS men helped him load the lorry. He was anxious to make the return journey that evening because a trip by day was a hazardous affair and risked the attention of Allied fighters which continually straffed the roads north of the front. Telephone communication with Milan was almost impossible, so he could only wait—and while he waited he too was filled with unease. His orders were to protect Mussolini, but more importantly, to see Mussolini did nothing politically unwelcome.

And Kisnatt, although he had believed Mussolini when he promised to remain in Milan, now felt less confident. He could only hope that the situation in Milan would not have suddenly changed by the time he got back.

It was a hope that was not to be fulfilled.

Twenty-five miles to the north of Milan, Rachele Mussolini was doing her best to comfort her children. They had arrived during the morning of April 25 at the Villa Montero in Cernobbio on Lake Como. The village is a resort with many splendid houses and hotels overlooking the serene waters of the lake and across to the town of Como, only a mile away. But on that dull day in April, most of the villas were empty. The German district commander and his staff, who occupied one of the big hotels, had gone and the tiny main street echoed with the noise of Wehrmacht vehicles on the move.

Rachele had come to Cernobbio that day from Lake Garda, on her husband's instructions—she and the two children, Anna-Maria, aged fifteen and Romano, seventeen—with the vague hope of crossing into Switzerland. The border was only five kilometres away from Cernobbio, but the family was stranded. The petrol for the big Alfa-Romeo in which they travelled had failed to arrive and no one in her escort of militia knew where to get any. The children were restive and Rachele could get no response when she tried to put a telephone call through to the Milan Prefecture. She talked to the children and tried to take her mind away from the great, uncertain void ahead of her. Slowly, the day passed.

No such problem of killing time burdened the mind of Walter Audisio that day. On the contrary, there was much to do. Milan, the centre of events in northern Italy, was too big a prize to let go by default, and this thirty-four-year old steelworker turned resistance fighter was determined that when the partisans took over the city, the Communist-led Voluntary Committee of Liberation would have the major share of power. It was a time for opportunity: a time for extracting revenge for the years of hiding and suffering and the fear of capture. It was a time of big rewards for the bold, a time when a man could claim a share of the glory.

And for Walter Audisio, alias Colonel Valerio, the moment to stake that claim was very near at hand.

The man they called Pedro slept fitfully in the meagre shelter offered by a tumbledown stone hut high in the mountains. Across his lap lay a British Sten gun with a full clip of 9-mm. ammunition in the breech. It was fully cocked. Even in sleep, his lean brown fingers held the gun ready, his finger touching the trigger guard. He was wet because a fine drizzle seeped through the broken roof of the hut and slowly soaked his rough, patched clothes. His soft peaked cap, with the five-pointed red star, was pulled down over his eyes. He breathed deeply as an exhausted man will, and the nerves of his body twitched. Occasionally he woke suddenly, turning his head in a watchful arc around his hideout before shifting his uncomfortable position and slipping again into a shallow sleep. He was relatively safe in the mountains and there was time for a little rest. Tomorrow, he would have to go down again to the lake.

Cardinal Ildefonso Schuster, Archbishop of Milan, had about him the air of a man on the brink of achievement. His gaunt features, normally so impassive, were now lit with a glow of quiet excitement and he moved busily about the offices of the Archbishopric in constant consultation with a stream of callers. And as far as he could tell, his ambitious scheme was moving smoothly to a logical conclusion.

For the fruits of his hard work during the first three weeks of April was to be the surrender of all German armed forces in Italy to the Italian Committee of Liberation for Upper Italy—a surrender brought about by the good offices of the Cardinal. The signatories to the surrender—the SS General Karl Wolff, overlord of Italy, and senior representatives of the Committee of Liberation—were due in the Archbishop's Palace in Milan on the afternoon of April 25. And the historic document was to be signed within the Palace precincts.

During the preliminary negotiations no mention had been made of Mussolini, nor of his government, nor of the Italian armed forces who were still fighting alongside their German allies. To the partisans, Mussolini no longer mattered, and to the Germans he was merely an embarrassment. If he knew nothing, he could do nothing; the war in Italy could be brought to a quiet end, and the Allies could do as they wished with Il Duce.

On the face of it, the Cardinal was on the eve of a triumphant coup.

But nothing in Milan during those days was quite what it appeared on the surface. For even when he was promising to go to Milan to sign the surrender, Wolff was actually crossing the border into Switzerland to conclude an independent surrender of German forces to the Allies. Wolff never did appear in Milan, nor did any of his staff, and at the end of what was to have been a historic day, Cardinal Schuster found himself merely the architect of a fiasco. It was typical of the confusion and disorder that existed everywhere.

For days, the Prefecture on Corso Monforte had been the vortex of this confusion. When Mussolini and his entourage had swept into the narrow arched gateway, Milan was still functioning as the principal city of Republican Italy. The shops were open, the trams ran and the industrial heart still beat. But slowly, the city was to collapse in disorder.

German troops guarded the key points in Milan and gave up the rest to the wave of insurrection that bubbled to the surface. By April 25, armed groups of well-organised partisans had occupied Fascist offices, and the opening shots in what was to become a fusillade of revengeful shootings had already begun. Shops began to close, the transport system seized up and, by afternoon, the sirens of the major factories like the Breda works and the Pirelli rubber plant wailed the signal for a general strike.

In the hiatus between power and imminent oblivion, the many who still clung to Mussolini scurried like worker ants backwards and forwards to the Corso Monforte. There were no longer police guards on the gates, and Birzer's stolid SS troopers had no interest in those who scurried, provided Mussolini did not leave.

Pathetic groups of the faithful came to stand in the courtyard and shout his name. Isolated squads of Blackshirts raised their

29

fists in the Fascist salute and swore their undying faith before the blank window on the first floor. Women and children stood in desolate groups, waiting to be told what to do. Cars nosed through the crowds and men from them ran up the steps leading to Mussolini's offices, shouting to others who ran down. Rumours ebbed and flowed on hoarse throats and noise swirled around the narrow courtyard and echoed to the grey sky in a bedlam of disorder.

And at the centre of it all was still Benito Mussolini.

For a week, he had held court in that first-floor office. A continual stream of visitors had flocked to him—ministers, diplomats, journalists, friends, Germans, Italians, soldiers, civilians, men and women, each with their own requests, advice, plans, questions, orders, messages and declarations. Entreaties to leave for Spain, for South America and Switzerland. Plans for a last stand, advice not to trust the Germans, pleas to discuss surrender with the partisans, messages of faith—he heard them all. To his callers, he revealed the whole spectrum of moods. Alternatively angry, placid, ebullient, depressed, vital and indecisive, Mussolini at one time displayed something of his old magisterial rage. For when his former Minister of the Interior Guido Buffarini-Guidi implored him to flee to Switzerland, he roared that he was master of his own fate: and then, an hour later, meekly promised Kisnatt that he would remain in Milan.

To a group of Fascist officers, he shouted defiantly that Fascism was immortal. He told them he would withdraw to the Valtelline mountains in the north with three thousand Blackshirt troops and continue the fight until he died honourably. But at the same time he anxiously sought news of tentative feelers being put out on his behalf towards the Committee of Liberation in Milan.

And while he seized eagerly on the ringing words of his Fascist Party Secretary Alessandro Pavolini, who guaranteed to lead an army to the Valtellina to fight to the last man, Mussolini was telling his Commander-in-Chief, Marshal Rodolfo Graziani, that he was arranging a meeting with the Committee of Liberation to find out their terms for surrender and so spare the Army further sacrifice.

And all the time the bad news of the military situation became worse. On Hitler's birthday, April 20, Mussolini faithfully repeated the rantings of his partner and spoke of new weapons and a turn in the tide of Axis fortunes. But he heard with dismay that Bologna had been captured. Two days later, Modena and Reggio fell, British troops entered Ferrara, while Cremona and Mantua were surrounded. On the same day, partisans rose up and occupied Genoa and Tito's troops had swarmed into Trieste.

Like some great cumbersome animal caught in the quicksand, Mussolini floundered, lashing out in all directions in the hope of a foothold. But there was none. The dictator of Italy, once courted and flattered by Adolf Hitler, had long been discarded and despised by his ruthless ally. Once, he had been the mediator of Munich, holding the peace of the world in his plump fingers; now the world no longer listened to him. Once, his armies had marched triumphantly through North Africa, to Abyssinia, into France and Yugoslavia and Greece, but now the victory banners had been trodden into muddy ignominy and the victorious parades of yesterday had turned into vast processions to prisoner-of-war camps. He who had ridden a white charger and intoxicated his countrymen with the power of his brave words was now being hunted by his countrymen. The erstwhile dynamic leader had become a rejected old man, three months short of his sixty-second birthday, with a bald head, a paunch, and yellow, haunted eyes.

3

Shortly before three o'clock that Wednesday after-noon, the frantic atmosphere in the Prefecture seemed more than ever divorced from reality. The sound of rifle fire snapping out somewhere across the city added an ominous note to the hubbub that arose all over the building.

Birzer took a last draw from his cigarette—his second packet of the day—and ground the butt beneath the heel of his jackboot. Slowly, he fastened the collar of his high-necked Waffen-SS uni-form, brushed his tunic automatically and walked out of his room, into a corridor and out into the courtyard. There, he spotted his second-in-command, Unterscharfuhrer Erich Guenther, standing with his arms folded, his peaked forage cap pulled down over his eyes, his gaze fixed on the main doorway of the Prefecture oppo-site him. From the doorway, a spiral staircase wound to the first floor, where the Prefect of Milan, Luigi Bassi normally had his offices. Now they were occupied by Mussolini and his entourage.

Birzer did not know Guenther well, but in the week since they had arrived in Milan, he had formed the impression that the lean, loose-limbed NCO was a good, sound choice for a right-hand man. Guenther saluted as Birzer approached.

"What's happening?" Birzer asked, indicating the windows opposite with a tilt of his head.

Guenther shrugged: "I wish I knew, So far, nothing."

But a moment later, a flurry of movement behind the windows across the courtyard alerted the two SS men. One of Kisnatt's SD men, in plain clothes, appeared at the window above the main entrance and waved to attract their attention. He pointed downwards, as if to indicate the door. Seconds later, Mussolini strode out and down the steps. Behind him, was the Prefect, Bassi, and Francesco Barracu, Under-Secretary of the Fascist Grand Council, a grey-haired veteran of Fascism and a man who was continually at Mussolini's side. The three men turned to their right and marched across the courtyard to the rear exit of the Prefecture, which led into an open garden. At the far end of the garden stood the barracks of the Milan Bersagliere. Mussolini led the way, his face set in a rigid frown, looking neither to his left or right. Barracu walked in step with him, talking all the time. Bassi strode along silently on Mussolini's other flank.

Faithful to his orders, Birzer began to follow the trio, telling Guenther to stay with him. Nobody had bothered to tell him of Mussolini's movements, but at that moment the German was not unduly worried for he knew of Mussolini's promise to Kisnatt not to leave Milan. But what nagged Birzer's orderly mind was the fact that he had no transport. Kisnatt had taken the SS men's truck with him to Gargnano. His first thought was that Mussolini was heading for the barracks perhaps to make a speech. For a moment, he lost sight of the three men ahead of him as they turned the corner of the barracks building, and he quickened his pace.

But as he reached the corner, he saw with horror that Mussolini was making for a large, red-brown Alfa Romeo limousine parked on the roadway just inside the barracks gate. What was more, the driver was obviously expecting him, for he held open the rear door until Mussolini climbed in, followed by Bassi and Barracu. Indecision gripped Birzer for only a moment—then he sprang forward towards the car. He was an athlete—he had an SS Silver Medal for athletics in his pocket at that very moment— but he never sprinted so fast as he did then. The driver, hurrying around the bonnet of the Alfa as Birzer broke into a flat-out sprint, had started the car engine.

There was no time for finesse. Birzer simply snatched open the rear offside door of the car and piled in, while Guenther lunged at the other door and tumbled inside. The two Germans sprawled in the back compartment breathless and sweating as the Alfa accelerated out of the barracks gate and swung sharply left. The momentum sent Birzer heavily on to Mussolini's lap. Enraged, Il Duce and his two companions screamed angrily and amid the confusion Birzer thought of pulling his Luger automatic from its holster on his right hip and ordering the driver to stop.

But Mussolini's rage subsided quickly, almost pathetically. As the apologetic Birzer raised himself, half-crouching in the back of the speeding car, Mussolini asked simply: "Who told you to come?"

"I'm sorry, Duce," Birzer replied. "But I have my orders."

No one else spoke for a few moments, and Mussolini stared out of the car windows. The streets of Milan, Birzer noted, were quiet. They were bare of traffic, but people still walked the pavements and he saw the occasional knot of armed German troops at street corners.

At length, Mussolini waved a hand towards the streets. "You see, Commendore?" he said. "I don't have to be afraid to go out on to the streets of Milan." Birzer made no reply. He badly wanted to know where the car was making for but decided not to ask. The best answer would be to arrive.

The journey continued in silence. Mussolini watched Milan recede with an impassive face. Dressed in the uniform of the Fascist Militia, a smooth-worn and well filled brief case between his feet, he seemed neither excited nor depressed. Only the ceaseless twitch of his podgy fingers betrayed his anxiety.

Birzer's legs were aching with the effort of keeping his balance in the low-roofed Alfa when the car turned from the street and stopped abruptly in front of an imposing building. Immediately, Mussolini opened the door and stepped quickly from the car, passing through a group of men obviously awaiting him at the door. Equally quickly, Birzer followed, but Mussolini gestured him away with a flick of his arm and the SS man hesitated, uncertain, in the hallway. Barracu and Bassi swept past him, speaking in urgent but hushed tones with the group who met them. But Birzer was not to be deterred for long. Resolutely, he marched in the direction Mussolini had taken and mounted a staircase to the first floor. There, he saw a number of priests but Mussolini had disappeared.

With some difficulty, Birzer at last found his bearings. He was in the Palace of the Archbishop of Milan. Automatically, he removed his cap.

The telephone bell cut through the strained silence of the Villa Montero and Rachele Mussolini started in surprise. The young trooper of her escort militia picked up the receiver. "Milan on the line," he announced. Rachele snatched the instrument expecting to hear Benito's voice, but instead, found herself speaking to her eldest son, Vittorio. There was no news of any certainty, Vittorio said. His father had gone to the Palace of the Cardinal Schuster to negotiate. Everything was unsure. Reluctantly, Rachele made her goodbyes to her son and replaced the receiver. Romano and Anna-Maria were waiting.

Cardinal Schuster greeted Mussolini gravely and urged him to take a seat. Mussolini, sitting wearily on a sofa gave Schuster the impression of a man benumbed by an immense catastrophe. His face hung in utter dejection. The Cardinal tried to open a conversation, but it was one-sided and difficult, for Mussolini seemed wrapped in his own thoughts and replied only perfunctorily to the Cardinal's openings. Schuster indicated a tray bearing biscuits and a decanter of rosolio, and Mussolini accepted a small glass of the liqueur and nibbled at a biscuit.

Schuster then spoke of his appreciation of Mussolini's personal sacrifice in facing a life of imprisonment or exile in order to save the rest of Italy from ruin. This gloomy prospect aroused little response from Mussolini. The Cardinal drew the parallel between his fate and that of Napoleon. Mussolini put down his glass and remarked that his own empire of a hundred days, like that of Napoleon, was about to expire. They touched on the relationship between the Church and Fascism and only gradually did the talk turn to the present. After an aching silence Schuster finally asked what Mussolini intended to do and, in a rare moment of decision, Mussolini said he would dissolve his army and militia and, with three thousand Blackshirt elite, would retreat to the Valtellina and continue the struggle in the mountains.

Schuster replied solemnly. "Duce, do not have any illusions, I know how many Blackshirts will follow you. There will be three hundred rather than three thousand."

"Perhaps a few more," Mussolini replied. "Not many though. I have no illusions." And with that, the sudden flicker of defiance died. The two men returned to their halting conversation on history, the saints and God's forgiveness.

But while they passed the time of day, others arrived at the Palace. The National Liberation Committee, whose members had previously discounted Mussolini as the proper person with whom to discuss the surrender of Italian and German forces in Italy, had grown impatient. The SS General, Wolff, had failed to arrive in Milan and his representative in the city had become less and less convincing in his assurances that Wolff would turn up. Finally the Liberation Committee agreed to speak to Mussolini. There was, after all, no one else.

The Committee's delegation was led by General Raffaele Cadorna, son of a former Commander-in-Chief of the Italian Army and an old and bitter opponent of Mussolini and Fascism. With him were two others, Achille Marazza and Riccardo Lombardi. The three men were ushered into an ante-room and received by the Cardinal's secretary. Don Giuseppe Bicchierai.

After a few introductory moments, they were shown into the room where Mussolini sat with the Cardinal. For the first time Mussolini came face to face with his enemies—men whom he had once dismissed as "a band of ruffians." They were to talk: he was to listen. It was a situation to which Il Duce was unaccustomed.

He stood in the background when the Cardinal rose to greet the three men. Schuster held out his hand, palm down, and each bent to kiss the ring on his finger. Having observed this ritual, Schuster introduced Mussolini. Nervously, Mussolini held out a hand, his face etched in a smile. With a glance at the Cardinal, Cadorna shook hands briefly with his enemy. Marazza, a lawyer by profession, who was at the meeting to represent the Christian Democrat party, touched hands with Mussolini without a word. Finally, Lombardi, of the Left-Wing Action Party, shook his hand.

There was an embarrassed silence in the study as Schuster sat down on a sofa and Mussolini took a place beside him. The others remained standing. It was just after six o'clock.

Waiting outside the apartments, Birzer found the vigil an agonisingly tense interlude. The moment he had lost sight of Il Duce, he became filled with the dread that he had been duped. It occurred to him that Mussolini might have left by another exit and with what at any other time would have been unseemly haste, he made a dash along the corridor taking the stairs two at a time until he reached the main door. There, to his relief, he found the reliable Guenther. Briefly, he instructed the NCO to hurry back to the Prefecture and bring to the Palace as many men of the SS squad as he could cram into their only transport—Birzer's personal Volkswagen Kubelwagen. Guenther sprinted away, seized the first bicycle he saw, and pedalled grimly through the streets back to the Prefecture.

At the time, Birzer had no idea what was taking place in the Palace, except that Mussolini was engaged in some kind of negotiation with the partisans. But that was worry enough. If anything happened to Mussolini, he reflected, his own future was unlikely to be a long one.

At about a quarter to six, he noted with relief the arrival of the Italian Army Commander and Minister of Defence, Marshal Graziani, accompanied by two SS men. They told him Graziani had been summoned to the Palace by dispatch rider. Confused and desperately worried, Birzer now warned the SS men to keep their eyes open and he went back again to the main door to await Guenther's return.

Rodolfo Graziani, the handsome, silver-haired soldier who led the Italian armies in their initial victories in North Africa, arrived at the Palace with another Minister of the Mussolini government, Paolo Zerbino, the Minister of the Interior. Within minutes of their arrival, Cardinal Schuster's secretary, Don Bicchierai, revealed that the Germans for the past two months had been negotiating for the surrender of their forces in Italy. It was now apparent to Graziani that the Germans had been living a lie in their relations with the Mussolini government and the realisation dumbfounded him.

It was in this dazed state that he was ushered into the Cardinal's study to join the negotiations. In an atmosphere of embarrassment and suspicion, the talks began. Here, in the city which had been the powerhouse of his ambitions, the scene of many of his personal triumphs, Mussolini had now come near to the end of his reign. Schuster was the first to break the silence. "Shall we sit here?" He indicated a large oval table in the centre of the room and ushered Mussolini into the seat on his right. Cadorna, Marazza and Lombardi sat on the left of the table. Graziani, Zerbino and Barracu faced them. The Marshal, with four rows of medal ribbons on the left breast of his tunic, gazed intently at the table, his face a mask of anger.

The Cardinal turned then to Mussolini, indicating he should open the proceedings, and for the first time, Mussolini looked directly at Cadorna.

"Well," he snapped, "what are your proposals?"

But it was Marazza who replied. His instructions, he said, were clear. "I have come here to ask for and to accept your surrender." In the silence that followed this cold demand, he added that he could allow only two hours in which to receive Mussolini's answer, since at the end of that time, the signal was to be given for a total uprising of partisan forces.

With the colour rising in his face, Mussolini angrily interrupted. "I'm not here for this," he shouted. "I come to discuss conditions ... to safeguard my men, and their families. What is to become of them? The families of the members of the government must be given protection. And I was also assured that the Militia would be treated as prisoners of war—"

"Details," Lombardi interjected. "Those are details, which we have the authority to settle here."

Mussolini looked sharply around the table as if to pursue the subject, but as quickly as his anger had risen it subsided and his mood of apathy returned.

"Very well," he murmured. "In that case we can come to some agreement."

The discussion proceeded and each point seemed to be resolved to the satisfaction of both sides. The Liberation Committee delegates assured Mussolini that the Fascist Militia would be treated in accordance with the rules of war relating to prisoners: the families of Fascists would not be victimised.

The subject of war criminals was then brought up. But suddenly, Graziani, who up to then had taken no active part in the talks, leapt to his feet and blurted out what he had learned about the plan for a German surrender from the Cardinal's secretary.

The shock of this outburst hit Mussolini like a physical blow.

Cardorna, with his eyes intently on Mussolini's haggard face, took up the theme and spelled it out in slow, measured words. "We have been discussing the terms of the surrender for the past four days," he said. "We have already agreed the details. We are expecting news of the signing of the treaty at any moment."

Mussolini remained speechless and as if in pain.

Marazza drove home the final barb. "Have they not bothered to inform your government?"

At this, Mussolini exploded. "Impossible!" he shouted. "Impossible! Show me this treaty."

But Zerbino confirmed that he too had been told of the imminent surrender. Mussolini was seized with ungovernable rage. He leapt to his feet and snarled that he had been betrayed.

"Germans!" He spat out the word. "The Germans ... they have always treated us like slaves. Now they have finally betrayed us."

Both Graziani and Schuster tried in vain to calm him, but it was clear that the negotiations were at an end. Mussolini marched across the room, declaring he was now free to act on his own. He threatened to broadcast to the Italian people and tell them of the German perfidy. Turning to the Committee of Liberation he said that an answer to their demands would be given in an hour. He strode from the room and Cardinal Schuster hurried after him. He wished Mussolini a safe return within the hour, but to this Mussolini made no reply.

Mussolini's exit from the Palace was a precipitous, angry gesture. Followed by Zerbino, Bassi, Barracu and a number of others, he swept past Untersturmfuhrer Birzer towards his car, his every step an essay in fury. Perplexed, Birzer piled into his Kubelwagen and followed the Alfa-Romeo back through the streets of Milan to the Prefecture.

There, the confusion was incredible. The courtyard resembled a disturbed ants' nest and as the cars bringing Mussolini and his entourage and Birzer's men drove into the courtyard, they were engulfed in a morass of humanity. Ministers and their families, members of their secretariats, Italian soldiers, journalists, a handful of war veterans, Blackshirts and a detachment of Fascist youth swarmed around the entrance to Mussolini's offices. Others packed the windows overlooking the courtyard and as Mussolini drove in, a great shout exploded around him.

Still burning with rage and humiliation, Mussolini strode through the main entrance and up the staircase to the first floor. As he stormed into his office suite, his anger finally boiled over. The target of his abuse was a Milanese industrialist, Gian Riccardo Cella, who had arranged the meeting with the Cardinal and the Committee of Liberation. The moment he spotted Cella standing amid the crowd of officials and Ministers, Mussolini trembled with fury and his voice rose to a piercing scream.

"Traitor!" he shrieked. "You deceived me, you led me into a trap. You'll pay for this with your life."

The outburst momentarily stunned the onlookers, but worse was to follow. In his office Mussolini found the German General

Wening, commander of the Milan garrison. Wening had come to the Prefecture to offer Mussolini an armed escort to supplement the SS bodyguard, but he had no chance to speak. Mussolini rounded on him, swearing and cursing and shaking his fist in the German's face. The Germans were traitors, he bellowed. General Wolff had betrayed him. He would rather die than accept an escort of filthy Germans. The General, who towered over Mussolini by nearly a foot, stood rigidly to attention during this diatribe. Then Mussolini contemptuously ordered him to leave the room, and, clicking his heels he left without a word.

Still uncontrollable, Mussolini then ordered everyone to go and he slammed the door of the office, leaving those outside wondering whether Il Duce was about to shoot himself with the pistol they knew he possessed.

His son Vittorio was one of the first who dared to re-enter the room. Mussolini had spread a large-scale map of Northern Italy over his desk, and he yelled that he was leaving Milan and would go to Como. Vittorio interrupted to remind his father that it was still possible for him to escape from Italy by plane, but Mussolini brushed aside the idea. Leaning across his desk he roared "You will not tell me what to do! I shall meet my fate here in Italy!"

Slowly, his anger subsided, but he still smarted at what he considered had been an attempt to trap him. Marshal Graziani then entered the office and informed Mussolini that he intended to withdraw his troops to the Como area. Mussolini appeared almost disinterested. "Very well, we shall go to Como together," he said. But soon he returned to the theme that burned in him. Two years before, he recalled, he had been arrested and imprisoned when leaving an audience with the King. "Now," he told the Marshal, "an attempt has been made this very night in Milan to put me in the bag together with the whole government."

Any further contact with the Committee of Liberation—still waiting in the Cardinal's Palace for Mussolini's answer—was now abandoned. Mussolini's fear of a trap seemed to be confirmed when a breathless messenger burst into the Prefecture with the news that partisan elements who had joined the Committee delegation proposed to shoot Mussolini even if he did agree to an unconditional surrender.

Ignoring a spate of advice from his Ministers who by now had crowded back into his room, Mussolini gave orders for a withdrawal northwards to Como and then to the Valtellina. Almost in a state of panic, Ministers, party officials and others who clung to the crumbling edifice of Mussolini's power, rushed from room to room, shouting orders, arranging transport and collecting papers, money and vital possessions for the journey. In the middle of it all, Alessandro Pavolini reiterated his promise to bring three thousand men for the last stand of Fascism in the mountains.

The rumour of this imminent departure reached Fritz Birzer's ears after he and Guenther had shouldered their way through the milling crowd to reach the office which they had commandeered. At once Birzer gave orders for his men to check their weapons and ammunition, gather together their equipment and prepare to leave in full battle order. The lack of transport was mitigated by the offer of an Italian Army truck, which Guenther had wrung out of the commander of the nearby Italian barracks.

In the middle of these preparations, an Italian officer burst into the room, telling Birzer that Mussolini wished to see him immediately. The SS man followed the Italian back across the courtyard and into the main offices. There, Birzer sensed an atmosphere of impending doom. In contrast to the wild excitement outside, here at the centre of the vortex, men walked quietly along the corridors. Others stood talking in urgent whispers. Some were slumped in chairs. One man was crying. Of them all, Mussolini himself seemed relatively composed—but he had in his eyes the strange, over-bright glitter of a desperate man.

Birzer saluted.

"Commendore," Mussolini said in his fluent German. "We are leaving."

This confirmed Birzer's worst fears. If Mussolini left now, before Kisnatt returned, he, Birzer, was left with the entire responsibility for his safety. He felt a shiver of fear running through his body.

"May I ask you, Duce, where you are going?"

Mussolini indicated the map on his desk. "To Como, and then to Merano."

"When do you wish to leave, Duce."

"Immediately."

Birzer tried to appear impassive, but his mind raced as he endeavoured to appreciate the situation. While his brain whirled, sifting facts and seeking solutions, he realised that Mussolini was saying something and tracing a route on the map spread before him. But Birzer was not listening any more. He knew that Mussolini's departure from this last stronghold would plunge what little order remained into pure anarchy. Furthermore, the already difficult and worrying task of guarding Mussolini must become virtually impossible.

And at the back of Birzer's mind was the menace of the Fuhrer's decree that soldiers who failed in their duty or deserted their positions would be punished by reprisals against their families. This threat could become horribly real. Birzer had a wife and two sons at home at Tosenheim, just outside Munich.

With mounting desperation, Birzer played for time. He reminded Mussolini of his solemn promise to remain in Milan until Kisnatt returned from Gargnano. Ought not they to wait until the SD man got back?

Mussolini gazed at Birzer for a moment or two.

"Times," he said at last, "have changed . . ."

Times indeed were changing—more quickly than Mussolini could have foreseen.

On that Wednesday, April 25, the mightiest concentration of arms the world has ever seen—the vast armies of America, Russia, Britain and their allies—were poised for the final knife-thrust into the heart of the enemy.

In the West, falling back across their own soil, entire German armies had almost ceased to exist. After a winter of savage fighting, Montgomery's British and Canadian forces had slogged through Holland, across the Rhine and were now streaming over the North German plains to within a hundred miles of the Baltic. South of them, General Hodges' US First Army had reached the River Elbe which neatly divides Germany north to south. There, after ten months of fighting all the way from the shores of Normandy, they met advance units of the Russian Marshal Konev's First Ukrainian Army. East and West joined hands.

Further south still, the flamboyant American General Patton's tank crews were resting before resuming their virtually unopposed drive into Czechoslovakia. It was now no more than a motorised advance and their greatest problem was coping with masses of prisoners. The US Seventh Army, under General Patch, had nearly reached Austria, while De Gaulle's joyous Free French armies, after so many years of waiting, at last carried the war into the homeland of their bitterest enemies.

And in the east, spurred on by memories of twenty million comrades who died in the savagery of four years of war, the Russians had gained the greatest prize of all. The race to Berlin between the armies of Marshal Konev and Zhukov had been a dead heat. Now, the steel nutcracker around the city was being squeezed hard. Courtyard by courtyard, block by block, street by street, Russian infantry moved towards the Reich Chancellery building. Across the ruins of the city, over the bodies of some of Nazi Germany's best troops, who had died to defend the Fuhrer, over the bodies of old men and boys thrown into the battle with only uniforms to identify them as soldiers, the Russians crept forward a mere two thousand yards from the Fuhrerbunker, where Adolf Hitler waited for the inevitable.

That day, Hitler had decided he would remain in Berlin. He had believed he was betrayed by the Germans who were, in reality, still dying for him. So he would die by his own hand.

And in the south there was total collapse. When the Allied armies in Italy—depleted though they were by the greater demands of the West—launched their attack across the River Po, they won the last battle. Before the power of General Mark Clark's US Fifth Army and the British General Sir Richard

McCleery's Eighth Army, Vietinghoff's German armies fell back in headlong retreat. Vast quantities of armour, guns and transport were abandoned and long caterpillars of prisoners clogged the roads southward. Only brilliant but isolated rearguard efforts held up the advance to the key cities of Genoa, Turin and Milan, while the way to the Brenner Pass and Austria was wide open.

As Mussolini prepared to pull out of Milan, American troops had already penetrated further north, their advance units heading for Lake Garda, the last seat of organised Fascist power.

Unlike Mussolini, the German hierarchy in Italy had come to terms with reality. Within four days, they were to sign the agreement for unconditional surrender of their forces in the Italian theatre of war, and by that time, Mussolini's fate was sealed.

For the third time that day, Yuone Fancelli set out from his room on Viale Padova for the Prefecture. Although still technically a serving trooper in the Decima MAS, he had discarded his uniform. He wore the tunic, but with identification marks removed, and a pair of old workman's trousers. Hidden inside his shirt he carried his service paybook, printed in Italian and German. Fancelli had been proud of his uniform and of serving Il Duce. He had believed in him to the last. Even though his own father was sent to Dachau for his resistance to Fascism and Nazism, twenty-year-old Fancelli, still unaware of his father's fate, had clung to his belief in Mussolini. It was, however, the wrong time to demonstrate it by wearing a uniform. Separated from his unit, he had come to Milan because Mussolini was there, but at the Prefecture had found a situation he had known once before. When Mussolini had been arrested by his own people in 1943, there had been the same confusion, the same hopelessness, the same automatic resignation to the force of events. Fancelli was willing to help, to fight if necessary, but he had found nobody prepared to give an order or to explain. Like thousands of other Italians, he had melted away from the crowd to hide and to wait and see.

45

Yet something drew him towards the headquarters of the man who had so inspired his youth that at seventeen, he had gone to enlist. Throughout the day, he had been back and forth to the Prefecture, always asking the same questions, demanding to know what was happening, what he should do. But always there was the same shrug of the shoulders, the same rumours. Now, for the third time, he set out to walk to the Corso Monforte. The time was a little before seven in the evening.

The sound of machine gun fire echoed from the distance and the occasional lorry-load of armed civilians passed along the long straight streets of the city. Milan was no place to be caught by enemy forces. Anyone in any kind of uniform was suspect to the bands of marauding partisans, who did not hesitate to shoot first and enquire later. Equally, the Germans, trigger-happy and nervous, were just as likely to open fire on anyone they thought to be a partisan.

Fancelli reached the Prefecture shortly after Mussolini had returned from the Cardinal's Palace. He elbowed his way towards the main entrance to the Prefect's offices, engulfed in a deafening clamour of voices. An Italian officer ran out of the building and began to barge through the crowd. They yelled at him to tell them what was happening. He replied that they were going north to Como. Everyone would know soon, he said. Fancelli grabbed the officer by the arm.

"Are you sure Mussolini is going north?" he demanded.

Importantly, the officer replied. "I have been given orders. We are going with Il Duce to the Valtellina."

Fancelli left the Prefecture as quickly as he could extricate himself from the crowds and ran to the Decima MAS barracks about a mile away. Here too, was an atmosphere of seething chaos. Several lorries and a number of cars were drawn up in a line and people were throwing luggage into them in frantic haste. The driver of one of the cars was filling the petrol tank from a can. Fancelli approached him, asking the soldier where he was going.

"Como," the man replied.

"Why Como?" Fancelli persisted.

"God knows," said the soldier. "But that's where Mussolini is going."

Fancelli made up his mind. He got into one of the cars, an Alfa-Romeo, where two women and five soldiers were already sitting. Nobody questioned him. He noted that the soldiers in the car had no insignia on their tunics. Was it with this band of refugees, Fancelli asked himself, that Mussolini was to make his last stand in the Valtelline mountains?

4

Mussolini erupted from the doorway of the Prefecture and paused as if to breathe in the yells from the crowd which greeted his appearance. The drama of the moment seemed to revive him, and he had missed nothing in making his exit a theatrical one. He wore his accustomed uniform—black shirt, grey tunic, breeches with twin red stripes down the sides, jackboots and a plain grey uniform forage cap. In one hand he carried a well-filled briefcase and cradled in the other arm, a machine gun.

Sternly, with his jaw thrust forward in the familiar manner which was the Mussolini image, he waited until the clamour had subsided and then, with an actor's perfect timing, uttered a last, hollow, command:

"Forward, to the Valtellina!"

"Duce! Duce! Duce!" they thundered.

A blind veteran of war was led to him and, with tears streaming from his sightless eyes, he pleaded with his leader not to leave. Others, who had waited so long for a decision, now joined the voice of the blind man and begged Mussolini to remain. Louder still, others shouted their undying faith.

Above the noise, Alessandro Pavolini, the man who was to bring the three thousand men to fight in the Valtellina, raised his arms and shouted: "Form the columns. We march!"

A squad of Blackshirts forced a path through the crowd for Mussolini who slowly approached the tangle of vehicles drawn up in the courtyard. Behind Mussolini struggled his secretary,

Luigi Gatti and an old contemporary of Mussolini's, Nicola Bombacci. Years before, these two men had been schoolmasters and then propagandists for revolution. They had split when Bombacci embraced Communism, but had become reunited now in a bond of common failure.

Following close behind in the cortège came most of Mussolini's Ministers. They, along with the Army and all other adherents to Fascism had been solemnly released from their oath of allegiance by Mussolini. But, useless gesture though it was, it changed nothing for them. There was no other way to go, except northwards with Mussolini. It represented the last hope of escape from the retribution which was drawing relentlessly around them. Zerbino, Romano, Liverani, Mezzasoma, the ex-minister Buffarini-Guidi, Tarchi—all were doomed men. And at least one had an accurate premonition. Asked where he thought they were all going, Mezzasoma shook his head in despair and muttered, "Perhaps to our deaths."

But now, as they pressed forward towards their vehicles, there was at least the impetus of action which brought its own excitement and sense of purpose. The hysteria of the past week had now given way to a relative calm—even though it would not last for long. Before the convoy moved away, Untersturmfuhrer Birzer fulfilled the ritual of his duty by reporting to Mussolini that the Waffen-SS 2/2 Flak Abteilung was ready to move. Mussolini nodded in acknowledgment, and Birzer withdrew. At that moment, he prayed that the dented, wheezy old Italian lorry which Guenther had procured for his squad would hold out long enough to get them to their destination, wherever that was. Guenther had grave doubts, but it was the best they could do and it was loaded with drums of petrol, kit, weapons and twenty of Birzer's men.

The convoy moved slowly through the crowds in the courtyard. Mussolini sat in the open Alfa-Romeo, flanked by Bombacci. On the bonnet, Gatti crouched with a machine gun in his hands, wrapped in a huge black leather jacket. Close behind came Birzer in his Kubelwagon and the SS lorry, the cars of the Fascist Ministers, lorries crammed with their possessions and most of the treasure looted from Government vaults, two carloads of Kisnatt's SD men, and, finally, driving his own car, Vittorio Mussolini. Towards the rear of this bedraggled convoy came a car with Spanish diplomatic number plates. Inside was Marcello Petacci and his family and, wrapped in a fur coat, Clara Petacci. Her days of waiting were over, and she was, as she had been determined to do, following her destiny with Mussolini.

As they emerged from the Prefecture, the caravan was joined by other vehicles, Yuone Fancelli's amongst them. There was also Wilhelm Hurtmanns, one of the few who left the Prefecture that day who would witness the climax of Mussolini's last journey and the hideous scenes in the Piazzale Loreto. Hurtmanns was a lieutenant in the 699 Panzer Propaganda Korps, a man who had, as a propaganda officer, recorded the victories of the German armies in the Balkans, Greece, Crete and with Rommel and the Afrika Korps in North Africa. He had also taken part in the long slow retreat through the desert and Italy. He went along with Mussolini's party now because he had been cut off from his unit in the general retreat northwards and wisely decided that for a German officer in uniform, there was safety in numbers.

The convoy unwound itself from the disorder of the Prefecture like a strand of wool pulled from a tangle, and it threaded its way through the streets of Milan—a long and ill-assorted cortège for the living. Mussolini busied himself with his despatch cases and rarely looked up as he passed through the strangely quiet streets. It was now dusk, and the skies above Milan were dark with cloud—a dismal, ominous night for the men, women and children who were now fleeing into the unknown.

Behind them in the Prefecture they had left only a skeleton of authority, including Pavolini, who was to leave to fulfil his promise of recruiting three thousand Blackshirts; Piero Pisenti, the Minister of Justice; and the Prefect, Bassi. The rest were melting away. The faceless crowds, the police, the Prefect's secretariat vanished in little scurrying groups and soon, where there had been noise, bustle and the clatter of feet, there was now only the whisper of an April breeze. The Prefecture, the last bastion of Fascist power, was almost deserted.

Across the city, in the Archbishop's Palace, General Cadorna, unaware of the exodus, awaited with mounting impatience some message from Mussolini. The Duce had said he would return in an hour and now almost two hours had already elapsed with no news from the Prefecture. Other partisan leaders turned up at the Palace, demanding to know what was happening. In the ever-present confusion, the simultaneous uprising of all the partisan and anti-Fascist forces in the city had not gone according to plan. Only odd groups, each with their own objectives and motives, had taken to the streets and the plans for the orderly take-over of power in the city had degenerated into a fragmentation of armed rebellion—a situation in which individual jealousies, bickering, and factional rivalry overshadowed the intended purpose.

At long last Cadorna demanded that the Prefecture be contacted by telephone, and a call was put through just after eight. The Prefect of Milan, Bassi, answered the telephone and blandly informed the Committee of Liberation that there would be no further negotiations and no surrender on Mussolini's part. He had quit Milan. Those gathered around Cadorna were staggered by the dramatic turn of events and it was precisely at this time that the ultimate fate of Mussolini was decided. Some leaders of the partisan movement were determined not to allow Mussolini to fall into the hands of the Allies. Mussolini was answerable only to his own countrymen. Alive he would be an embarrassment to the country, to the Allies, to everyone.

One who strongly shared this view—because of his hatred of Fascism—was Walter Audisio. Given the opportunity, he would have no hesitation as to the course events must take. And within forty-eight hours, that opportunity was indeed to be presented to him. Fate had set Walter Audisio and Benito Mussolini on a collision course.

As darkness fell over Lake Garda, Kriminalinspektor Kisnatt was at last ready to make a move. American and British aircraft, which had been a deadly menace to anything moving on the open road, had now left the skies and he was eager to be on the way back to Milan to re-establish contact with Mussolini. He climbed into his car and headed west, ordering the lorry which he had loaded with files and belongings, to follow. By the time they had cleared Gargnano, it was late and he could not hope to be in Milan until the middle of the morning. But once there, Kisnatt could have some influence on events. Or so he hoped.

As Fritz Birzer drove the Kubelwagen through the northern suburbs of Milan in the wake of the Mussolini caravan heading for Como, he was deep in thought. A perfectly ordinary Unter-sturmfuhrer—the colourfully titled SS rank was equivalent to lieutenant in the rest of the German army—Birzer now found himself the senior German officer with responsibility for the security and safety of Mussolini. Wryly, Birzer reflected how rapidly events had unfolded. A week ago, Mussolini had been safe in Garda, surrounded by barbed wire fences, battalions of SS, the omnipresent and always rather sinister SD and all the other elements of a super-security system. Now, there remained only himself and twenty-two men to keep vigil over the departing dictator. An even more disturbing circumstance—and one of which he had become aware only in the last couple of hours—was the increasing hostility of the Italians towards him and his men.

There had been sporadic shouts of "Traitors!" in the Prefec-ture but now Birzer sensed a sudden change in the attitude of the Italians. They felt they could at last openly demonstrate their resentment of the Germans since there was nothing to lose. As soldiers, Birzer regarded the Italians as beneath contempt, but nevertheless they were well armed and if it came to an open fight, Birzer was in jeopardy. His men carried Schmeisser automatic rifles, he had a machine gun and in the lorry was an anti-tank weapon and a heavy machine gun. The SS were good fighters and Birzer had confidence in his squad. With Unterscharfuhrer Guenther leading them, their morale was still high and their military bearing and discipline were conspicuous amid the confusion and disorganisation of the Italians. Nonetheless, the SS were heavily outnumbered.

He could depend on his men but could he depend on Mussolini himself? Birzer was unsure, and his uncertainty was not lessened when he discovered the route it was intended to take. Como was only a few kilometres from the Swiss border and if they proceeded along the west bank of Lake Como the border became even closer. The more he dwelt on it, the more he was convinced Mussolini might try to elude him and head for Switzerland. He vowed not to let Mussolini out of his sight for a moment, even if it meant staying awake for the next week.

The journey northward to Como was achieved without incident. The only interruption occurred about half an hour after leaving Milan, when a German artillery unit, retreating north, blocked the road and forced the convoy to stop. Birzer sprang from his car to sort out the problem and demanded to see the senior officer. To his surprise, he was introduced to a General whose name he could not catch, although he at once recognised his rank. Birzer explained the nature of his journey and the General asked to be introduced to Mussolini. He expressed surprise that the convoy was going along the western shore of Lake Como, since the area was known to be alive with partisans. For a few minutes, Birzer entertained the hope that the unknown General might persuade Mussolini to take an alternative route to the north, away from the partisans and, more importantly, away from Switzerland. He hurried back to the convoy and spoke to Mussolini. Without demur, the Italian leader agreed to meet the German General and accompanied Birzer to him. While Mussolini and the General talked, Birzer struck up a conversation with an artillery officer who said the artillerymen were taking the east road round the lake.

"Pity we can't join you," Birzer said.

"Glad you're not going to," replied the artilleryman. "We've got enough troubles of our own."

To Birzer, it was a chilly reminder of the responsibility which lay on his overburdened shoulders. Mussolini returned some five minutes later, nodded to Birzer and indicated that they should proceed. There was to be no change in the plan.

Like the unknown artillery unit which had delayed them, there were many other Wehrmacht groups on the road of retreat that night. Night was the only safe time to travel since by day the Allied air forces had complete domination of the air over northern Italy. And one such group was a convoy of thirty-eight trucks belonging to a Luftwaffe communications unit. Heavily laden with telephone and telegraph equipment it was under the command of Luftwaffe Oberleutnant Fallmeyer. It was heading for Como and Fallmeyer was concerned only in getting his unit towards Austria and out of the war zone intact. He knew nothing of Mussolini or his entourage and yet, within thirty-six hours, the stocky Bavarian Luftwaffe-man was to play a key part in deciding the time and the place of the dictator's death.

Mussolini's column reached Como between nine-thirty and ten that night. The town was busy with traffic since the German garrison in the surrounding area was preparing to pull out. The line of vehicles turned off the main roads and streamed through the narrow streets around the Prefecture of Como. The cars containing the Ministers pulled into the courtyard, together with the SD cars, and unloaded their occupants into the cramped square.

Mussolini who now seemed revived, sprang from his car to trot briskly up the steps of the Prefecture to the left of the arched main entrance. Inside, he was greeted by Buffarini-Guidi, the ex-Minister who lived near Como, the Prefect Celio, and a number of Fascist functionaries including Paulo Porta, the Inspector of the Fascist Party in Lombardy. The Prefect's wife scuttled away to prepare a meal of some sort for her guest, while Mussolini and his followers crowded noisily into a reception room on the first floor to begin their arguments all over again. As always, the proponents argued their cases at the top of their voices and the din only subsided when the telephone rang and someone snatched up the instrument to hear the latest situation from Milan.

The news was bad. The vacuum they had left had been quickly filled. The Americans were on the city outskirts, armed bands of partisans were shooting Fascists without trial, roads out of the city were being blocked and the Germans were abandoning the city and joining the retreat to the north. And if the incoming news was bad, the answers were equally depressing. Minister of Popular Culture Fernando Mezzasoma had tried desperately to get news of Pavolini and the Blackshirt loyalists he had promised to gather together. He made repeated telephone calls, the last to the offices of the newspaper *Corriere della Sera*. Curtly, he was informed that the newspaper had been taken over and the offices were occupied by partisans. It was, even for these desperate times, a depressing picture.

As was now his habit when things were running against him, Mussolini withdrew into a mood of dark brooding, illuminated only occasionally with a flash of defiance. He refused food but listened to the insistent words of Buffarini-Guidi who urged him again and again to take the chance to escape across the Swiss border at Chiasso, where the Swiss and the Italian frontier guards would let him through without opposition. It would be so easy, said Buffarini-Guidi persuasively, for them to make the short journey by car. Half an hour, and they would be on Swiss soil. Marshal Graziani, however, poured cold water on the idea. He had been in touch with the German garrison commander in Como, he said, and had been assured that flight into Switzerland was out of the question. The Swiss would not allow him to pass across the frontier.

Porta, the Fascist chieftain in the district, declared brusquely that it was futile of them to wait any longer for Pavolini. They must press on north and await the Blackshirts there. For a moment, Mussolini was roused by this suggestion.

"I shall go to the mountains with Porta," he declared. "Surely it is not possible that I cannot find five hundred men to go with me?"

He wanted to know from the others what they thought, and so the quarrelsome dialogue droned on towards midnight without any decision.

Outside, Untersturmfuhrer Birzer sat hunched in the back of the Kubelwagen, parked with the SS lorry outside the street entrance to the Prefecture. Previously, he had walked into the courtyard and checked for himself that there was no rear entrance. Then he called his whole unit to attention and addressed them.

"Two sentries will be posted on the gate throughout the night and until further orders," he began. "Unterscharfuhrer Guenther will detail you. I must be told immediately—immediately—there is any sign of movement, and particularly if you see Mussolini making any preparations to leave. The rest of you stay by your vehicles. You may smoke if you wish and you had better eat some field rations. But on no account will you accept food or drink of any sort—even water—from an Italian. You understand? Nothing! I wouldn't put it past the bastards to try to poison us."

He then checked the four big drums of petrol stacked inside the lorry and gave instructions that none of it was to be sold or given away except on his direct orders. "Don't let me catch anyone giving as much as a spoonful to an Italian," he added. Thereafter, Birzer made another check on the Prefecture, satisfied himself that Mussolini had gone upstairs to the Prefect's office on the first floor, and spoke to the group of SD men gathered around their cars in the courtyard. They were a worried bunch, Birzer noted, and it gave him an odd satisfaction. The Sicherheitdienst were policemen, Gestapo agents, spies even on their own countrymen, even amongst the armed forces and they were universally disliked and feared. At Gargnano, the SD, with their fearful power had been masters of everything. How different they were now.

Birzer asked if there was any news of Kisnatt. One of the SD men, who had tried vainly to telephone Milan, said there was no information. Birzer returned to his car, lit another cigarette and waited.

At about the time Mussolini's car was drawing into the Prefecture in Como—about nine-thirty that Wednesday evening—a small group of men were trudging doggedly uphill through the trees which grew on the mountainside some thirty miles to the north. Four of them were lean and weatherbeaten and they moved with the light footfalls of those accustomed to walking in the mountains. The fifth man in the party laboured hard as he walked and the others paused frequently for him to rest a moment to catch his breath. The four were Italian partisans. One of them had trained as a lawyer, another was a fisherman, the other two farm labourers, but they had long since given up their occupations to live and fight in the mountains overlooking Lake Como. The fifth man was a Swiss businessman named Alois Hofmann, who lived in the village of Domaso on the lake below where they now walked. For months past, Hofmann had helped the resistence men by passing on information about German and Italian troop movements and other snippets he picked up in his travels around the lake, largely unhindered because of his Swiss passport. But during March he had aroused the suspicions of the German police and despite that he was a sick man, he had fled from his home, taken to the mountains and had been found by the partisans.

The leader of the partisans was a young man of twenty-four, of slight build, with a black pointed beard and dark brown thoughtful eyes. His name was Count Pier Luigi Bellini Delle Stelle, descendent of a family of Florentine noblemen. Mussolini had come to power the year after the Count was born. Bellini had taken a degree in law at Florence University and, with the restrictions imposed by the war, had found a job with a bank in his home town. But now, on this cold, damp April night, Pier Bellini, son of nobility and graduate in law, was better known by his battle name—"Pedro," the tough, resourceful commander of the partisan group called the 52nd Garibaldi Brigade. For his skill in mountain fighting and in weaving a collection of fishermen, shepherds, peasants and farmworkers into a highly efficient battle force, Bellini had been given command of the 52nd, a unit also known as the "Luigi Clerici" in honour of a former commander, killed in action against the Germans.

A measure of his effectiveness as a partisan leader was that Bellini had been given command of one of the Garibaldi Brigades (named after the statesman who united Italy as a single state) even though he was not a Communist. Few non-Communists were placed in key positions in the active arm of the partisan movement which was almost entirely Communist controlled and organised.

It had been a bad winter for the partisans. Units like the 52nd Brigade were in existence despite a proclamation from the Allied Commander-in-Chief in Italy, General Alexander, telling them to disperse for the winter, implying that they could expect no further help or supply drops. One of the reasons for this was the acute shortage of supplies available in Italy, such was the demand of the armies in the West. However, with considerable determination and a great deal of improvisation, the partisans carried on. But it had been far from easy. German and Italian pressure against them had increased. An offensive at Christmas, 1944, had taken a heavy toll of the 52nd Garibaldi Brigade, cutting its fighting strength from forty to a mere twenty-five men, thinly spread through the mountains.

Nonetheless, they were still tying down German and Italian troops in considerable numbers, maintaining nightly patrols and attacks, in particular, sabotage raids on the main railway line running north from Milan to Lecco, up the west shore of the lake and ultimately to Austria and Germany. They used hand grenades—captured in raids and harvested from the bodies of their enemies—to blow up the electric power stations feeding the line. It might not have been a mighty blow for freedom, but at least they had the satisfaction of slowing the freight trains that ran north each night loaded with plundered equipment useful to the German war effort.

Their armoury resembled a war surplus store, consisting of British, American, German, Italian, Belgian and French weapons ranging from old, long-barrelled rifles made well before World War One, to modern British Stens, the weapon Bellini himself favoured. He carried one this night, as he walked steadily uphill to the comparative safety of a clump of trees half a mile above the lake.

The morrow was to be a big day for Bellini and his men. It was one of the two days in the month when the shops in the village distributed a meagre supply of tobacco and all-important salt. In his pocket, already written out and sealed with the small rubber stamp of authority he carried with him, was a formal receipt for half a kilo of tobacco and a ration of salt. Payment would be made when the war ended. Until then, the shopkeepers of Domaso and a dozen other villages on the lake were content to comfort the partisans on credit. And there was little enough comfort. Since the Christmas offensive, the men of the 52nd had slept rough, no longer able to use the tiny stone shepherds' huts in the hills which had previously been their homes. Now, against the increasing skill of their enemies, they had to keep on the move. Each man carried with him a couple of blankets slung round one shoulder—enough to keep out some of the cold and some of the heavy dew. Sleep was something which came only with total exhaustion.

Bellini had been a chunky 160 pounds when he took to the hills in June 1944. Now, he weighed no more than 100 pounds and had learned to live with hunger. He had concluded long before that civil war was the worst kind of all, and he conducted it sorrowfully. For him it was not even an ideological fight, but simply a means of bringing back some kind of peace, sanity and rule of law, which, paradoxically, he had so often violated and yet held dear.

It was that thought which was to guide many of Bellini's actions during the next few days.

Rachele Mussolini lay fully clothed on her bed in the Villa Mantero gazing at the ceiling and reflecting with bitter sadness on her separation from her husband, a separation which seemed now to stretch away into infinity. The children were asleep near her and it was on their insistence that she had lain down.

Benito was now in Como. This she had heard from the Militia, some of whom now slept on the floor near her. But what was to happen to him, to her, to the children? Outside the window, she heard the sound of trucks rolling along the road. It was the last of the German garrison in the little town pulling back into Como.

At about two in the morning she was suddenly startled at the sound of a footstep at the door of the villa, followed by the low murmur of conversation. A minute later, a Militiaman tip-toed into the room.

"There is a letter from Il Duce," he whispered.

Rachele leapt from the bed and snatched an envelope from the young soldier's hand. Excitedly, she ran to the bedside lamp and tore open the envelope. She took out a single sheet of paper, recognising the red and blue pencil which Mussolini used for his private correspondence. In his spiky scrawl, he had written:

"Dear Rachele, I have come to the last phase in my life, the last page in my book. Perhaps we shall not meet again. That is why I have written this letter I ask your forgiveness for all the wrong which, involuntarily, I have done you. But you know that you are the only woman I have truly loved. I swear this to you before God and before our Bruno at this supreme moment. You know that we must go to the Valtellina. You, with the children, must try to get to the Swiss border. There, you will make a new life. I think they will not refuse you entry, because I have helped them in every way and you have nothing to do with politics. If this should fail, you must give yourself up to the Allies, who will perhaps be more generous than the Italians. I commend Anna and Romano to you, particularly Anna, who has most need of your care. You know how much I love them. Bruno from the height of the sky, will help us. I embrace you and the two children. Your Benito. Como 27 April, 23rd Year of the Fascist Era."

The text of the letter was written in blue, the signature in red.

The two children had clustered around their mother as she read. Now, she handed the letter to them and told the Militiamen to try to make telephone contact with the Prefecture in Como. She sank into a chair, tormented with the premonition of disaster. When at last the call was put through to the Prefect's offices in Como, Mussolini's secretary Luigi Gatti answered it. Rachele assailed him with questions, but after a short time, she heard the telephone taken from him and her husband's voice, deep and melancholy.

"Rachele! At last . . . your voice . . ."

They exchanged greetings with the tenderness which Mussolini always seemed to hold for his wife, despite the years of his infidelity and the violent, plate-throwing quarrels that erupted frequently whenever Rachele was reminded of the presence of Clara Petacci. Now, he begged her to take the children with her and find shelter in Switzerland

"But what about you?" Rachele wanted to know. "You must find a place of safety. Our safety is nothing compared to that."

"Me? I am alone, Rachele." His voice was doom-laden, apathetic in a way which even she had rarely heard before. "Even Cesarotti, my chauffeur has left me . . . but you, you must take the children somewhere safe. I can only repeat what I said in my letter. Forgive me for all the harm I have done you . . . your life might have been so quiet and happy without me. I have always loved you, and you know it."

Desperately, Rachele tried to cheer him up. "There are plenty left who are ready to fight for you. You have lots of followers left, and those around you will do anything for you."

"But there is nobody left," he cried. "Rachele, I am alone, and I can see well enough that everything is finished."

He then asked to speak to the chief of the guard at the Villa Mantero, and reminded him of his duty to care for the family. Then he spoke to the children. Romano begged his father not to leave them, but Mussolini told him not to be afraid and gently bade both the children goodbye.

Then Rachele spoke again and Mussolini said goodbye to her, too. "You must make a new life, Rachele," he said. "Lose no time. Goodbye, Rachele. Goodbye."

Rachele heard the soft click of the receiver being replaced at the other end of the line.

In the Prefecture, Mussolini walked slowly back to the Prefect's apartments. The arguments had abated for a while and now some of the Ministers, like Graziani, tried to snatch a little sleep on sofas and armchairs. Buffarini-Guidi had left. Porta was still holding forth about the need to go north immediately. And still there was no news of Pavolini and the men who were to make the last stand of Fascism.

Further depressing news continued to reach Mussolini. A truckload of papers, personal and official, which he had carefully sifted from the files in his offices in Gargnano had failed to arrive in Como. The truck was to have followed him from Milan, and its non-appearance agitated him. About midnight, he dispatched Gatti and his adjutant, Colonel Vito Casalinuovo, to take the road back towards Milan and find out what had become of the truck. When they returned with their tidings, Mussolini was plunged into gloom. The truck had been captured by the partisans.

Those still on their feet discussed the latest events in low voices. Mussolini himself was immersed again in the endless sorting of papers and documents which he fished out of his cases. He read them with the aid of glasses which had now become necessary to him, although he hated to be seen wearing them.

The great march to the Valtellina had, it seemed, become the echo of a dream.

At the height of his power, Mussolini enjoyed addressing cheering crowds from balconies facing onto public squares as in this scene at Palazzo Venezia in Rome. (UPI photo)

Clara Petacci, Mussolini's mistress.

His wife, Signora Rachele Mussolini (at a Fascist Youth Parade in 1936).

In Milan before the last journey, Mussolini's drawn and haggard face reflected his awareness of approaching doom. With him is Fascist Party Secretary Alessandro Pavolini.

This mutilated image of Mussolini, fixed by a sword to a tree in Messina, foretold in 1943 of Il Duce's downfall. (National Archives)

Dongo—seen from the road as it curves round the massive rock known as the Val'Orba. This was as far as the convoy carrying Mussolini got.

Mezzegra—it was in this gateway that Mussolini and Clara Petacci were shot. Two crosses on the low wall mark the spots where they died.

Mussolini's corpse rests upon the body of Clara Petacci after their execution. (National Archives)

The grim display of the bullet-ridden corpses of Mussolini and his retinue attracted thousands of people to the filling station. (UPI Photo)

In Milan, the dead body of the fallen dictator and his mistress were strung up on the girders of a gasoline filling station. (UPI Photo)

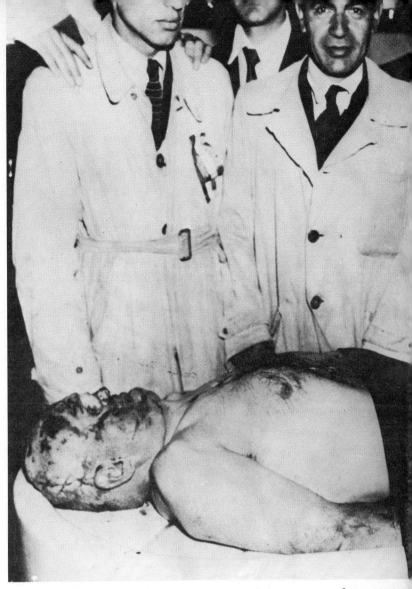

Even after Mussolini's body had been removed to a morgue, crowds of unsorrowing citizens gathered to view the remains. (UPI Photo)

Pier Bellini delle Stelle, commander of the 52nd Garibaldi Brigade—the partisan unit which captured Mussolini at Dongo.

Walter Audisio—known as Colonel Valerio—the man who shot Mussolini and Petacci one afternoon at Mezzegra.

Aldo Castelli, holding the Luftwaffe overcoat which
Mussolini was wearing when captured.

In 1947, two years after his death, almost 20,000 people assembled in the ruins of the Basilica di Massenzio, to hear Walter Audisio affirm that he "executed the Duce" by order of the Partisan Command. (UPI Photo)

Satisfaction with the part they played in the capture and execution of Mussolini and other high-ranking Fascists is evident in the faces of three other partisans. (UPI Photo)

5

Otto Kisnatt looked anxiously at his watch. In the dark, with the roads wet under the sizzle of the tyres, he had not made good time on the journey back to Milan and, as his driver negotiated the outskirts of the city, it was already nearly three o'clock in the morning. Milan had about it a ghostly air, even for that hour. Nothing stirred on the roads in the south-western suburbs as the SD man at the wheel drove towards Corso Monforte.

Suddenly, rounding a corner, the driver cursed loudly and rammed on the brakes, jerking Kisnatt from his worried thoughts. "What the hell . . ." he snarled angrily.

"Couple of drunks lying in the road," apologised the driver.

Kisnatt peered through the mud-spattered windscreen and saw two bodies lying in the road. Kisnatt got out of the car and walked carefully towards them. With the toe of his shoe, he prodded one of the figures and, getting no reaction, he bent down for a closer look.

In the headlights, the driver watched Kisnatt's face—the Kriminalinspektor's black toothbrush moustache gave him an uncanny resemblance to Adolf Hitler—as he peered at the two men in the road. At last Kisnatt walked back to the car.

"They're dead," he said curtly. Both the men were stone cold, lying in their own blood. It was a grim welcome to Milan.

"Drive to the Prefecture—quickly," he ordered. The driver skirted the two unknown corpses and raced through the streets towards the Prefecture. Both iron gates were wide open when they arrived. There was no guard and the courtyard was deserted. There were lights on at some of the windows of the Prefecture, but everything was wrapped in chilly silence.

Fighting the panic that threatened him, Kisnatt leapt from the car and bolted through the front door of the main office block. Not a soul was to be seen. He took the stairs three at a time and arrived on the first floor. The last time he had been there, he had had to push his way through a milling mob. Now, there was no one. He stopped in the corridor leading to Mussolini's office and called out. A cat darted across the corridor and startled him, but there was no answering voice.

Pulling the automatic from his pocket Kisnatt advanced towards the door of the office, hesitated a second, then threw it open. The room was empty. Back in the corridor, he pocketed the gun and clapped his hands together and hollered again: "Hello! Hello!"

Only his own voice echoed back.

He ran out of the building and across to the ground-floor offices where Birzer had stood twelve hours before and where the SD detachment had also set up an office. All was deserted. Frantically, he ran back to his car and ordered the driver to make for the Muti barracks at the back of the Prefecture, where his squad had been quartered. Here at last were signs of life. A truck was parked outside, and in the guard room, Kisnatt found the Italian commander, a Colonel, in the process of packing a case ready to leave.

"Where's Mussolini?" Kisnatt demanded of the startled Colonel.

The Italian shrugged. "I'm not sure. There's been a general strike in the city . . . the National Liberation Committee have taken over the government . . ."

Kisnatt did not wait for further explanations. He ran out of the room and up the stairs leading to the men's quarters. The room was empty, with every indication of having been evacuated in a hurry. Tired and dispirited, Kisnatt began to retrace his steps to his

64

office where he sat for some time, racking his brain in an attempt to fathom the situation.

Then he saw the note lying on his desk.

"Today, 25.4.45 at 20 hrs, we departed for Como." The message, written in obvious haste, was signed "Lange", the Hauptscharfuhrer who was Kisnatt's senior NCO.

Kisnatt stuffed the note into his pocket and bolted from the room, calling for his driver.

Elsewhere in Milan at dawn that morning there was activity. Pavolini had managed to assemble a force of men who—at that stage at least—were willing to give some substance to his strident claim that he could muster an army. There was by no means the three thousand he promised, and before long, many of those would disappear. But this at least was a start. As they assembled in more cars and lorries on the Via Mozart, the Party Secretary seemed ebullient and confident.

In one of the cars was a girl in her early twenties, with long blonde hair. A woman of indefatigable energy, she had insisted on Pavolini providing her with a car to make the journey to Como with this sad remnant of Fascist might. Soon she would be near Mussolini and remain close to him until nearly the end. Her name was Elena Curti Cucciati. She was the daughter of one of Mussolini's former mistresses, Angela Curti, and it was widely alleged that the Duce was, in fact, her father.

At about three-thirty on the morning of Thursday, April 26, the Prefecture at Como suddenly came to life again. Marshal Graziani, who had been resting on a sofa, woke to find the offices in turmoil. Luigi Gatti was rounding up those Ministers still present and urging them to hurry. Il Duce was leaving Como.

Graziani found Mussolini still wearing his grey Militia uniform and the insignia of an honorary corporal—Hitler was the only other holder of the rank—which he valued so much. Graziani asked him where he was going.

"To Menaggio," replied the Duce crisply.

Menaggio, on the lake shore thirty-six kilometres north of Como, was the most important town of the mid-lake district. It was the landing point for the ferry that connected with Varenna on the eastern shore of the lake which at that point was little more than three kilometres wide. It was also a junction with the lakeside road and another which ran up through the steep hills, across to Lake Lugano—and Switzerland.

Graziani said he would take Mussolini to his car and he would meet him later in the day at Menaggio. Nicola Bombacci joined them in the office as they waited to depart, while officials, Ministers and soldiers overflowed into the courtyard, now crammed with vehicles and men. Outside, Untersturmfuhrer Birzer had momentarily left his car to stretch his aching legs. Then, out of the night air, he heard a shout from the Prefecture gateway. It came from one of his sentries.

"Herr Untersturmfuhrer! Quickly!" Birzer was at the entrance arch within seconds. The agitated sentry pointed into the yard.

"They're trying to leave. They've surrounded Mussolini's car and they're keeping the SD back," he cried.

Birzer could make nothing of the milling shadows in the courtyard in the dim light shed from the windows of the offices. Then he spotted the bulky figure of Mussolini with Graziani towering over him. Dozens of men were gathered around them while others formed a line behind his car, screening it and preventing the SD car from following.

"Fetch the Unterscharfuhrer and four others at once," Birzer ordered the SS sentry. "And tell Schultze to park my car across the entrance."

The sentry doubled away to tell Guenther and instruct Birzer's driver to move the Kubelwagen. Birzer waited until Guenther came running with four SS men, all armed with automatic rifles, then he walked forward into the glow of light. In his hand he held his own machine gun with the safety catch still on. When the SS squad appeared, all voices were stilled into a pervasive and ominous silence. Mussolini stood by his car, watchful like the rest. But none of the Italians made any attempt to move away from the SD car. It was a silent trial of will which Birzer knew he had to win if he was to stand any chance at all of staying with Mussolini. He took a grip on his gun and waved it to indicate that the Italians should move aside. No one moved. Birzer wondered what would happen if he carried out his orders to the limit and shot Mussolini. He played the next card in his slender pack.

"Entsichern!" he shouted. It was the German command to release safety catches and he hoped Mussolini would understand. He heard the simultaneous click of five weapons.

"Durchladen!" he commanded. Instantly, the SS men worked the breeches of their guns to put the first bullet in the firing position. Six automatic weapons now pointed into the crowd in the courtyard. One more word from him would be enough to unleash slaughter in that confined space. His men would obey without question if he gave the order to fire.

But the rattle of the gun breeches was enough. The Italians melted. A little shaken, Birzer lowered his machine gun, slipped the safety catch on and walked towards Mussolini, still well covered by his men. Mussolini stood still and calm, apparently unmoved by Birzer's display of determination.

Birzer saluted. "Now we may proceed, Duce."

But Graziani cut in furiously. "Out of the way," he roared. "Il Duce can go where he likes."

As calmly as he could, Birzer clicked his heels and replied. "Not without an escort, Marshal. Those are my orders."

Turning to Mussolini, Birzer repeated: "You must not leave without an escort, Duce."

Mussolini gestured wearily to those around him, indicating that they must accept the inevitable.

"Very well, Commendore," he said. "Very well."

Birzer saluted again and stepped back, waving to the four SS men behind him to withdraw from the courtyard. With his machine gun slung over his arm, he watched the small crowd of men swirling around Mussolini, who still stood near the doorway leading into the Prefect's office upstairs. In an odd way, he felt sorry for the man. His gesture of resignation had been so pathetic, so charged with defeat that Birzer felt the sense of pity a man has for a trapped animal which has no longer the will to snap back at his captors.

It started to rain shortly before three o'clock in the morning of Thursday, April 26, just as Birzer heard the sound of the cars in the yard being started up. He waited until he was sure Mussolini was in his car, then walked across to his Kubelwagen, climbed in beside his driver, Schultze, and ordered him to pull behind Mussolini's car when it appeared.

Mussolini told his entourage that he would go on ahead to Menaggio and there wait for the rest of the convoy—and perhaps Pavolini—to join him. Graziani watched Mussolini, accompanied as ever by Luigi Gatti, his secretary, climb into a car. The Marshal, weighed down with a sense of approaching doom was alarmed when those still left in the Prefecture raised an incongruously spirited shout of acclaim to their departing leader: "Duce! Duce!"

Graziani turned resignedly to one of his aides: "Now everyone knows where Mussolini is," he sighed, watching with an impassive face as the cars in the courtyard filed through the big dark archway into the wet streets of Como. The tall, wavy-haired Marshal had long been burdened with doubt about the journey that Mussolini was now taking, and already he was inclined to abandon the futile flight and return to his proper place, the headquarters of his army. Nevertheless, he began issuing orders to continue the journey, at least as far as Menaggio.

In the drizzle, the six or seven cars carrying Mussolini, Gatti, Porta, Zerbino and a number of others Fascists twisted and turned through the narrow streets of Como and headed for the lake road. Birzer was in the middle of the procession, followed by the lorryload of SS men, two cars of SD and the sumptuous Alfa-Romeo driven by Marcello Petacci. And in the back of the Alfa sat Clara Petacci. She wore a big fur coat, several rings on her fingers and a complete make-up. She might have been going to the opera. It was typical that she would remain well groomed even on her way to a rendezvous with fate that was to bring her short but privileged life to an end.

Within fifteen minutes of leaving Como, the entourage reached Cernobbio and plunged into the dark narrow street which cut through the lofty old houses of the town like a gorge, and passed the Villa Mantero without stopping.

The villa, as Mussolini probably well knew, was deserted. An hour before, Rachele and the two children had left the house with the escort of Militiamen and had driven to Como. From there, their car turned on to the road to Chiasso on the Swiss border in an attempt to carry out Mussolini's last instructions to her. As the car topped the rise in the road over the mountain ridge which runs parallel to Lake Como, Rachele saw below her the lights of Switzerland. They gleamed like diamonds on a cushion of velvet, strongly contrasting with the drab, wet darkness of Italy where the lights were blacked out by wartime regulations.

As it drew near to the frontier barrier, Rachele's car was halted. An Italian officer approached and said he had been sent by Il Duce to see her safely across the border, only a hundred metres away now. The road was full of vehicles, and among them, to her surprise, Rachele thought she saw that of Buffarini-Guidi, although there was no sign of the ex-Minister himself. She held her identity documents and those of the children in her hand as the car rolled slowly forward to the frontier. Only five metres from the freedom of Switzerland and the new life which Benito had urged her to make, she waited while a Swiss customs official studied her and her documents. He took the papers away and after a wait of about half an hour, he returned, saluted and shook his head. The Italians around Rachele began to argue, but the Swiss remained adamant.

"Absolutely impossible," Rachele heard him say, and sank in her seat, sadly recalling her husband's last words—"they will not refuse you."

She gave instructions for the car to be turned back, and once they were heading towards Como, Rachele felt oddly relieved. At least in Italy, she would be better able to keep in touch with her husband, and there was still the possibility of joining him on the road north. Approaching Como, the roads were congested with traffic. It was nearing dawn, and the journey was held up frequently by convoys of German army trucks filing through the town and by Italian cars going in all directions. And there was a renewal of a far more sinister activity. The sound of rifle fire, which had so frightened her the night before, had now begun again. The partisans, it was said, were coming down from the mountains in force. The Villa Mantero was dark when they entered the drive and Rachele decided to go to the headquarters of the Fascist Federation in Cernobbio, where it might be safer.

But there, the state of affairs was a microcosm of the situation throughout the country as the end drew near. Fascist officials hurried in and out of the building, clearly engaged in preparations for escape. Mussolini had left Como and gone north, they said. There was thus no point in staying any longer. The Americans had entered Milan and the partisans were swarming into Como extracting a terrible toll of vengeance on all suspected of being Fascist. Some asked Rachele what they ought to do but there wasn't any answer she could give. In her turn, she tried to find out where her husband was, but could get no clear information. The children sat on the stairs of the offices while she went to try to organise help but it was a futile effort. And then she discovered her car had been stolen. It was the last straw. Rachele Mussolini broke down and silently wept, as the dawn of a new day emerged through the mist of her tears.

Mussolini arrived in Menaggio at about five-thirty, having made slow time in covering the thirty-six kilometres from Como on the narrow, winding road hugging the lake shore and wriggling through dozens of tiny fishing villages—Moltrasio, Laglio, Brienno, Argegno, Mezzegra, Tremezzo, Cadenabbia—hunched beside the grey water. Even so, he had left the main body of the convoy, led by a lumbering armoured car and a few truckloads of Republican soldiers, far behind.

There were few people about in the little town when the leading group of cars halted beside a low building just beneath the level of the road. It was the office of the municipality. Opposite was the local school, which had been commandeered long ago for use as a barracks. Further along the road was the villa owned by the local Fascist leader Emilio Castelli and it was to this house that Mussolini made his way. Doggedly, Birzer shadowed him until he was quite satisfied Mussolini was settled inside—perhaps lying down to sleep—and then he posted sentries at the back and the front of the villa. He next set out to take stock of the town. The choice of a resting place filled him with his usual anxiety since a glance at the maps in his car had confirmed a growing suspicion in his mind that Mussolini would eventually make some attempt to shake him off and head for the Swiss border.

The road along which they had travelled from Como split into three at the centre of Menaggio. Straight ahead from the junction lay the main lakeside road. This was the road Mussolini had taken and it contained the schoolhouse, the town offices and the villa in which Mussolini was resting. To the right, another road led into the town square, formed a kind of promenade along the edge of the lake and rejoined the main road through the town about one kilometre further north. And to the left, climbing steeply uphill with sharp bends almost every hundred metres, lay the road to Lake Lugano and Switzerland.

A closer look at his map convinced Birzer that Menaggio was the last point at which it was possible to branch off to Switzerland until the northern end of Lake Como, where the road split again—continuing north into Switzerland, and turning east towards Merano through the steep wild mountains of the Valtellina.

By the time Birzer had finished his reconnaissance, the little town was filling with vehicles of all types. Led by a big armoured lorry with a heavy machine gun mounted on a turntable turret, a line of trucks and cars filled with men, women and children filed into the place, spilling the usual excitable groups of people arguing at the tops of their voices, while the local people looked on sullenly. In the middle of the crowd was Mussolini's secretary, the indefatigable Gatti, who, by means of enormous lung-power, was gradually winning an argument, urging the bulk of the entourage, together with the troops who accompanied them, to go back down the road towards the next sizeable town, Cadenabbia. It was stupid, he urged, to congregate in Menaggio with so large a gathering, since the whole world would soon know where Mussolini was. There was truth in the argument, but the result of Gatti's plea was to create further disillusion in the ranks of those who had followed so far.

"We came to die with Il Duce!" some cried. "And now we are being turned away."

Yuone Fancelli, the young Decima Mas trooper, was one of those turned away in Menaggio. He now rode with a truckload of soldiers. On the laborious journey from Como, morale in the truck had not been very high; almost without exception, the men had a depressing feeling of uncertainty. One man declared flatly that they were being led into a trap; another, that they would be left to fend for themselves since Mussolini planned to slip over the border into Switzerland and desert them. Some talked of going home and only rarely did anyone declare willingness to follow Mussolini wherever he went. And now, in Menaggio, they were being told to go back along the road they had just travelled.

Reluctantly, they reversed the trucks and headed back. Many did not stop at Cadenabbia, but kept on going and were lost from the scene. Almost every hour thereafter, they were joined by others—disillusioned, homesick, frightened, hungry and thoroughly demoralised. Fancelli himself stayed for just one more day.

And in the midst of it all, Untersturmfuhrer Birzer remained apprehensive. He hurried back to the Villa Castelli, for a further check with his SS sentries and there he saw Mussolini's adjutant, Colonel Casalinuovo escorting Clara Petacci into the house. But by this time, Birzer was aching with fatigue, drained by the continual tension of the past few days and the lack of food and sleep in the past twenty-four hours. Heavy-footed, he walked back to the school where the SS unit had found themselves quarters and where a camp bed awaited him. With a last instruction to Guenther to wake him if there was the least sign of movement from the Villa Castelli, he threw off his tunic and boots and fell asleep on the bed.

Five men rose from their resting place on the mountain at around five in the morning—about the very moment Mussolini was entering Menaggio. Here, high above Domaso, twenty-two kilometres north of Menaggio, it was utterly silent save for the hiss of the steady rain on the branches of the trees beneath which the partisans had spent the night.

Pier Bellini shivered, used though he was to the elements. He stretched his cramped legs and stood up. Softly, he called to the others and together they checked their weapons, wiping the damp from their guns and working the breeches as noiselessly as they could. Bellini asked if the Swiss, Hofmann, was fit enough to make the difficult journey downhill and they then set off in single file down the slippery track that led to the outskirts of Domaso. They walked steadily for an hour by which time the roofs of Domaso were directly beneath them. Bellini ordered two of his men to remain with Hofmann safely outside the village, while he and the remaining partisans filtered into the streets below.

Bellini had been on this dawn patrol many times before, but he never took risks. And the risks were considerable. Domaso was garrisoned by units of both Italian and German troops—the Italian Black Brigade unit quartered in a hotel in the village, and a company of German infantry stationed in a villa by the lake. And even though the Germans were mostly reserve troops, they were well armed and they heavily outnumbered the local partisan forces.

As Bellini approached the first houses on the inland side of the village some of the early rising inhabitants were already up and about. Normally the villagers greeted the partisans with wary warmth, paying due respect but careful not to make too much of it. But Bellini was completely unprepared for the welcome he now received as he walked down the first street. The excited populace swarmed around the young partisan shouting welcome, their faces alight with fervour.

"Viva partisan!" they yelled, clapping the bewildered Bellini on the back. "We are liberated! The war is over!"

It was some minutes before Bellini could subdue the babel of voices to ask what had happened and only with difficulty was he able to comprehend the chorus of excited replies.

"The Americans have entered Milan! There is a big uprising in the city! The Germans have retreated! The Fascisti have fled! The Germans have gone! The war is over!"

Alarmed at the noise created by the demonstration, Bellini managed to calm the villagers and isolate a young fisherman who had helped him previously and whom he knew to be reliable.

"Now, tell me quietly what has happened," Bellini insisted.

"We had news from Como," the fisherman replied. "There has been an uprising in Milan and the Americans have arrived there. The Fascisti have fled Milan and the Germans are in retreat."

"Is it true?"

"Yes, it must be. Here in Domaso, the Black Brigade are leaving. They are scared to death, you can see it on their faces."

"And the crucchi?" Bellini used the local dialect for the Germans.

"They're still here," the fishermen said, "but they're ready to run."

"They are, are they?" Bellini stood thoughtfully for a few moments. "Well, let's go to Mario's and find out."

Bellini walked warily with the fisherman to the cafe which stood in the main street of Domaso where he could sit, discreetly screened by an arched arcade facing the lake. There, while the proprietor fetched coffee and cigarettes, Bellini began shaping in his mind the beginnings of a plan of action, weighing up the

74

chances which he guessed were balanced delicately between success and complete disaster. Point by point, he went over the idea forming in his brain.

The news of the American occupation of Milan, the uprising and the flight of the Fascists and Germans, he decided, must be fairly accurate. Two nights before, on the radio hidden in the village school he had heard the latest war situation broadcast on the BBC Italian service. It was critical. So if the information he had just been given was right and the Italians and Germans in the lakeside area were ready to pull out, it was time for the 52nd Garibaldi Brigade to come out into the open and act.

There was also a matter of simple arithmetic. Scattered around Domaso, were some twenty-five regular partisans upon whom he could rely utterly. They were armed and ready and willing to fight. Against them were perhaps a hundred, maybe two hundred Italians and Germans garrisoned in the lake villages between Domaso and Dongo, six kilometres south. And there would be more Germans, in considerable numbers, on the other side of the narrow neck of lake spanned by the Ponte del Passo, north of Domaso.

If therefore it came to an open fight with the Germans they could have little hope of survival. On the other hand, if the Germans were unwilling to fight, words might well be better ammunition than bullets.

His first act was to send word to his second-in-command, a twenty-five-year-old engineer named Urbano Lazzaro, urging him to muster all the members of the 52nd Brigade outside the village and to bring with them the two heaviest weapons in their armoury, a pair of deadly accurate British Bren guns.

Bellini was about to embark on a gigantic bluff. It began with a sheet of cheap paper torn from a child's school book which Bellini had asked Mario to fetch him. Pushing aside the Sten gun lying on the cafe table, he wrote a formal letter to the Italian and German commanders of the Domaso garrison. The note contained both a preposterous demand and a massive lie.

In his careful, educated handwriting, Bellini wrote out a demand for the complete and immediate surrender of all troops in the face of an overwhelming force of armed partisans. He signed it and stamped it with the official stamp of the Luigi Clerici Brigade, then handed it to a young girl who had many times previously ran messages for the partisans on her old, pre-war bicycle.

Now, she pedalled away with the most crucial message of them all. Bellini calmly ordered another cup of coffee, cradled his Sten gun once more in his arms and waited for the commanders' response.

While he waited, Mussolini twenty-two kilometres away, slept soundly, unaware that a message on a scrap of paper was to prove part of his death warrant.

6

When dawn broke on April 26, Como was in a state of near chaos. As in Milan between the departure of Fascist power and the arrival of Allied troops there was a period of upheaval in which violence, confusion and uncertainty swirled through the town like fog. Partisans and others who had previously opposed the Fascist regime were joined by opportunists with guns in outbursts of shooting which turned most streets into rifle ranges. Amid the groups of fleeing Fascist officials there mingled Republican army deserters, regular troops with apparently no clear idea of where to go or what to do. There were also units of frantic German soldiers obsessed with the single aim of evading the American troops, now pushing towards the foothills between Milan and Como.

Into the middle of this morass drove Alessandro Pavolini heading a convoy of assorted army units from Milan. His car drew up outside the Prefecture and Pavolini and some of his staff vanished inside. The young Elena Curti Cucciati got out of her car and walked down the line of lorries towards the Prefecture, intent on finding news of Mussolini. But there was none. Il Duce had already left Como, someone said, and had gone north by the lake road towards Menaggio. He had left in the middle of the night and the rest of the Ministers had followed him.

By now the partisans were swarming into the town and no one knew for sure if the road to Menaggio was still open. Some said the town was sealed off by roadblocks; others, that the Americans were approaching. Everyone loyal to Mussolini, it appeared, had already departed; others, not so quick, had been rounded up and shot by the partisans. It was a wretched reception for a force already demoralised by the swiftly deteriorating situation of the past twenty-four hours, and now an air of despondency and irresolution descended over the whole enterprise.

Engulfed by this uncertainty and unable to obtain accurate information, Pavolini decided to try to contact Mussolini personally in Menaggio, so that he could report the situation of the forces he had promised to rally. He told Elena Curti Cucciati of his intentions and the girl quickly pulled her car into line behind the four others carrying Pavolini and his staff northwards along the lake.

But their departure was to prove a grotesque error of judgement. With their leader gone, harassed by forces far beyond their power to resist, the last hope of Mussolini's fighting rearguard gradually broke up. The men, the guns, and the equipment which might have prolonged the existence of the Duce's remnants were never to leave Como.

Only the promise still remained, and Pavolini took it with him on the dash to Menaggio, now made hazardous by the ever-present threat of partisans. His arrival in the town was watched with bewildered interest by the people who now crowded the streets, anxious not to miss a single movement in the drama being enacted in their little town in the first soggy hours of that rainy Thursday.

Pavolini's little cavalcade drew up outside the Villa Castelli at about nine o'clock. Like some conquering hero, the Party Secretary raised his arms to a crowd and they broke into a ragged cheer which swelled to a genuine chorus of greeting when Mussolini suddenly strode out of the house to greet his faithful lieutenant. With due solemnity, Pavolini in his blackshirt dress and Mussolini in his grey Militia corporal's uniform, embraced each other and then went inside the villa, followed by Elena Curti Cucciati and the little group of army officers and officials who had travelled with them. Mussolini greeted them all with vigour. It seemed as

78

if a brief rest had done him good. His demeanour suggested he had reached a clear decision.

But by then, other, far more fateful decisions had already been taken elsewhere.

Pier Bellini did not have to wait long for a reaction to the note he had sent to the Italian and German commanders. In a little over half an hour after she left the café, the girl on the bicycle came skidding up to the door, dropped her machine in the roadway and hurtled inside.

"The Italians have gone," she panted. "So I took the letter to the Germans and now the officer wants to see you."

Bellini, together with his second-in-command Urbano Lazzaro, a young partisan named Aldo Castelli and the Swiss Alois Hofmann, received the news with guarded optimism. It might be a trap, yet if he could talk to the German, with the aid of the multi-lingual Hofmann, there might be a chance his bluff could succeed. It was a risk worth taking.

"We'll go," he announced. Quickly, he briefed Hofmann. The Swiss knew the German commander slightly and it was therefore more likely he would believe Hofmann than a partisan. Bellini told Hofmann he must make it clear to him that the partisan force surrounding Domaso was a large one, well equipped and ready to annihilate the Germans if they refused an immediate surrender. Bellini then turned to Lazzaro, addressing him by his battle-name of "Bill".

"Bill, you go and spread the word—the moment anyone hears a gun fired, they are to come quickly." Lazzaro nodded and left. Bellini turned again to Hofmann.

"Are you ready?"

Hofmann hesitated: "What if they refuse to surrender?"

"In that case," the young partisan replied, "we're going to have a hell of a fight on our hands."

Bellini borrowed a white handkerchief from the Swiss and tied it to the muzzle of his Sten gun. Then he rose and walked slowly out of the café on to the main street. The waters of Lake Como, grey in the reflection of the overcast sky, lapped gently at the shore a few feet from the edge of the road. Otherwise, the street was quiet and there was little movement in the old, shuttered houses facing the lake.

Approaching the villa where the Germans had their headquarters, Bellini was joined by Lazzaro, while a couple of partisans with rifles waited in the street. There was no sign of movement from within the villa but the deputation was evidently expected. The gates of the villa were wide open and the sentries, when addressed in German by Hofmann, conducted the partisans to the office of the German commander, a middle-aged man whose rank badges, Bellini discerned, were those of a major. The German rose and bowed slightly and sat down again. An NCO stood behind him, watching the partisans warily.

Bellini nodded to Hofmann and the Swiss began explaining in faultless German that Domaso was entirely surrounded by a force of several hundred well-armed partisans preparing to launch an all-out attack on the town. The only thing that could prevent the total annihilation of the German garrison was unconditional surrender. Hofmann said he knew that the Italians had fled. The Germans were therefore isolated.

The German screwed up his face in an agony of indecision. Then he blustered that he could not surrender to an unauthorised force. It was unthinkable that a German officer should be asked to do so. There was still a war on. He would be shot for treason.

Hofmann translated but Bellini's reply was quick and decisive. He was in no mood to sympathise. "Tell him that we are a recognised force, and that our authority lies in the magazines of our guns."

The German took the point. Weary, beaten, hopeless, he signified his willingness to surrender. Both parties to the surrender signed a formal document which said that the Domaso garrison had laid down its arms before overwhelming force. For the German, the document was an insurance; for Bellini, it was a weapon.

The unit of fully-equipped German infantry then handed over weapons and stores to a handful of partisans. It was a complete victory, yet only the start of a sensational day for Pier Bellini and his men.

With the windfall of new weapons and ammunition, the partisans discovered still another prize; the German garrison was well supplied with petrol. Bellini knew of an old rusting Fiat owned by one of the villagers—a partisan sympathiser who had laid the car up for lack of fuel. Commandeering the vehicle he filled the tank to the brim and loaded it with reserve jerricans of petrol. Thus, at last, the 52nd Garibaldi Brigade was mobile and with that mobility, Bellini decided to extend his area of operations.

With Domaso firmly in his hands, he handed out the older rifles and carbines from his stock of weapons to any old man or boy capable of holding a gun and thus re-equipped his regular partisans with the new German guns just captured.

Bellini's aim now was to repeat his bluff further afield. To the north of Domaso were two more German garrisons, at the Gera Lario and, beyond the bridge at the north end of the lake, at Delebio. To the south, there lay two other lakeside villages, Gravedona and Dongo. But the bridge, Ponte del Passo, was the key to control of the north end of the lake. Hold that, Bellini reasoned, and the west side of the lake all the way down to Como was sealed off. Accordingly, he set off north in the old Fiat with Hofmann, Lazzaro and as many partisans as he could cram into the vehicle to repeat his bluff to the German garrisons at Gera Lario and Delebio. In his pocket, he held a trump card; the surrender document signed by the commander of the Domaso garrison. He had in mind nothing more than a holding operation once he gained control of the area. The overall strategy was to prevent the movement of German troops pending the arrival of Allied forces.

So far his boldness had paid off, but the biggest dividends were not to be yielded for another day or more.

About ten o'clock that same morning, the SS guards watching Villa Castelli in Menaggio saw Alessandro Pavolini hurry out of the house, climb into a car and drive off towards Como.

Soon, others left the villa and started piling their cases and other paraphernalia into the line of cars drawn up outside. It seemed like the preparation for a mass exodus and one of the SS men hurried down the road to the school house where his unit was bivouacked. He reported the activities to Unterscharfuhrer Guenther who at once roused Birzer, sleeping on a camp bed.

Birzer leapt up in alarm as Guenther's anxious voice reached him.

"Herr Untersturmfuhrer! Herr Untersturmfuhrer, they're moving." Guenther cried. "There are a lot of cars and it looks as if they're going to make off."

"Is he still in the house?"

"Yes."

"Thank God," Birzar muttered as he leapt from the bed, still wearing his breeches. He pulled on the coat handed to him by Guenther, forced his feet into his jackboots, buckled on his belt and holster and scrambled out of the building. The cold rain stung Birzer in the face as he ran towards the Villa Castelli with Guenther close on his heels. Crowds had gathered around the house and Birzer shouldered his way through. He had seen the cars Guenther had mentioned. There were five of them, all dark green and brand new Alfa-Romeos. He also noted that they were facing the wrong direction, not north, but towards the road junction at the south end of the town, where the road forked towards Switzerland.

Birzer prepared himself for another showdown. He sent Guenther back to the school to bring the Kubelwagon. Then he checked with the SS sentry outside the house. No, Mussolini had not appeared yet. He asked an Italian officer with gold braid on his shoulder where Il Duce was, but he didn't make progress with his bad Italian. A moment later, his question was answered when Mussolini himself strode through the doorway.

To Birzer's eye, there appeared to be a subtle change in Mussolini's bearing. He looked confident, almost arrogant again. Perhaps it was because of the presence of the elegant Clara Petacci. Whatever it was, Birzer determined to find out. He stepped up to Mussolini, clicked his heels and saluted.

"Duce, I must ask where we are going," he said, stressing the plural. But he was quite unprepared for the reply.

"Follow me," Mussolini snapped, "and you'll find out."

Saying that, he stepped past the nonplussed Untersturmfuhrer and hurried towards the line of parked Alfas. Petacci was still beside him and a bevy of Ministers, officers and soldiers followed in his wake. Birzer watched Mussolini step into one of the cars—the second or third in the line—when Guenther arrived with the Kubelwagen. Unfortunately, it was facing the opposite direction to the Alfas and as he ran towards it, calling the SS men to follow, Birzer caught a glimpse of a more ominous movement among the cars and lorries which littered the road. One of the big Italian armoured cars was pulling to the rear of the line of Alfas, between them and the Kubelwagen, strategically positioned to prevent Birzer from following.

But the SS man was not to be denied. Jumping into the driving seat as the alert Guenther shifted into the passenger seat, he rammed the scout car into gear and shot away down a side road, through the town square again to the main road. But by this time, the Alfas had pulled away. Birzer spotted them: they were taking the road to Switzerland.

Cursing everything around him, Birzer stamped on the accelerator and tore off in pursuit up the steeply rising road. Changing down, he made the tyres squeal in negotiating the first hairpin bend—and then he saw the armoured car again. It was lumbering along behind the Alfas, completely blocking the road. Birzer drove close behind and began to swing from side to side in a vain effort to pass. But there was no question of doing so. For one thing, the road was too narrow and twisting.

And for another, the Italian gunner in the turret on top of the vehicle swung a 20 mm. cannon point blank at the Kubelwagen.

There was nothing Birzer could do but fall in behind the armoured car. From time to time on the bends he was able to obtain glimpses of the green cars. At the end of the steep winding section of the road, the armoured car picked up speed and closed in on the Alfas. Birzer began to feel alarmed. What would happen if they reached the Swiss border? Should he carry out the last of his orders and shoot Mussolini? Should he act now and risk being blasted by the cannon on the armoured car? As these alternatives flicked through his mind, quite suddenly, a new problem was posed. Two of the Alfas now swerved off the main road and cut uphill on a small road to the left. As Birzer flashed by, he caught sight of them and of the remaining three cars, still speeding ahead of the armoured vehicle. Here was a dilemma. Which cars had pulled off? Was Mussolini in one of them? And, most vital of all, which road was the shorter route to Switzerland?

For a few more minutes Birzer drove on, then braked hard, swung the Kubelwagen round on the slippery road and headed back towards the two Alfas which had left the main road. This he felt was the road which led more directly to Switzerland. But it was a grievous miscalculation. The Swiss border lay directly ahead of him, some fifteen kilometres distant. Yet it turned out to be a fortunate mistake.

Birzer arrived at the side road determined that if there was to be a crisis, he was gong to meet it right there. He ordered Guenther and the other two men out of the car.

"Stay at this junction," he snapped harshly. "And if anyone at all tries to pass you—shoot to kill."

Birzer then drove as fast as he could back to Menaggio, where he found the 2/2 Flak Abteilung in battle order and ready to move. With them, he sped back to the crossroads. There, Birzer set up a machine gun post, using the heaviest weapon to cover all approaches to the side road. Then he and the rest of the unit advanced cautiously up the road which led steeply uphill to a large square building at a dead end. And outside the building—he later discovered it was formerly a hotel—were the missing Alfa-Romeos. Fervently hoping that Mussolini was in the building, Birzer advanced, signalling his men to spread out and surround the place. Inside, he heard the hum of voices and crept closer to a window on the ground floor from where most of the noise appeared to emanate.

And there, to his intense relief, was indeed Mussolini. He stood in the room amid a crowd of men and women, including Clara Petacci, talking in excited tones and, of course, in Italian, which Birzer was unable to understand. But the topic of their conversation was of little interest to him. It was enough to have caught up again with his quarry.

Birzer told his men to remain on the alert and he posted sentries around the building—the Hotel Miravelle. After a careful reconnaissance of the place he waited for the next move. It was certain now that Mussolini was considering a break across the Swiss border. There could have been no other reason for him to have left Menaggio. Birzer was resolved that Mussolini would not escape him again. From now on, he would refuse to follow the other man's dictates. From now on, Mussolini would move when he, Birzer, was ready. Angrily he stalked around the Hotel Miravelle, swearing at the rain which fell steadily from the slate-grey sky.

Kriminalinspektor Kisnatt at last arrived in Como after an exhausting drive from Milan at about midday, and it seemed he had struggled out of one disintegrating situation into another. Milan, when he left, had been in complete chaos and Como was now exactly the same. The air was full of the sound of gunfire and the clammy, almost tangible sweat of fear. The Prefecture, where Kisnatt made his first stop, was a vacuum of uncertainty.

When he demanded to know where Mussolini was, the frightened occupants shrugged their shoulders and said they had no idea. Some would not admit he had been there, others simply refused to speak. At last, Kisnatt cornered a police official and demanded to know what had happened. At first the man refused to answer. Beside himself with rage, Kisnatt yelled at the man threatening to shoot him if he did not tell what he knew. At last the scared policeman whispered that Mussolini had left for Menaggio at three o'clock that morning. Kisnatt dashed to his car, swearing with anxiety and eager to continue the crazy paper-chase which he hoped would lead him to Mussolini.

He was really only a few hours away from his fugitives but the irony of it was to be that when he did reach Mussolini, he was to be instrumental in delaying him—and thereby sealing off the last hope of escape.

Behind him in Como, Kisnatt had left Pavolini, still believing he could salvage something from a rapidly collapsing situation, and so fulfil his boast to bring three thousand men to the Valtel-lina.

Inside the Hotel Miravelle, the aura of hope, the brief effervescence which Mussolini had brought with him soon degenerated once more into despondency. More and more anxious men and women continued to arrive from Menaggio until the area outside the hotel was jammed with vehicles and the entrance and ground floor rooms were thick with talk and cigarette smoke.

The news from outside was as depressing as the weather. Milan Radio, seized that morning by the Committee of Liberation, was now pumping out a steady stream of war news, decrees, orders of the day and instructions to the populace. For the occupants of this last dreary stronghold of Fascism, it was an unending flow of disastrous news.

The flashes from the war fronts were bad enough. The Germans were now admitting that Russian artillery was shelling the centre of Berlin. From Allied communiques it was clear that apart from small islands of resistance, the advance of British and Americans and their allies through Germany was now virtually unchecked. And in Italy, the list of towns and cities falling into Allied hands read like an extract from a Michelin guide. Even the most optimistic among Mussolini's ever dwindling entourage could hardly ignore the fact that the end was drawing rapidly near.

But even more ominous news was to come. Among the unending bulletins issued by Milan Radio was a report of a proclamation in the name of the Italian people establishing popular courts of justice and tribunals to deal with war crimes. Exactly what that meant for the men huddled in the Hotel Miravelle was spelled out in Article Five of the decree. In both indictment and punishment, it was coldly unequivocal. Members of the Fascist government and the leaders of Fascism "who are guilty of suppressing the constitutional guarantees, destroying popular liberties, creating the Fascist regime, compromising and betraying the fate of the country, and conducting it to the present catastrophe are to be punished with the penalty of death, and in less grave instances, life imprisonment."

For Mussolini and those around him, it was a sentence of death.

And yet these men who now faced total disaster were seemingly unable to connect with reality. The two ends of the Rome–Berlin Axis, around which both Hitler and Mussolini boasted the rest of the world would revolve, had collapsed in utter chaos. But the preoccupations of the two dictators at this moment were quite removed from the dominant facts of their lives. Deep in the Berlin bunker, where the hollow thump of Russian shells echoed down the air ducts, Hitler was still issuing maniacal orders, manoeuvring phantom armies which had long ceased to exist, deploying troops who had died, been captured or given up the fight long before. Beyond all reason, he could now deal only in fantasies.

Mussolini's preoccupations were even more absurd. He was in the midst of a jealous quarrel with the fiery Clara Petacci and the young Elena Curti Cucciati. Cucciati had gone to the Hotel Miravelle with the others to await news from Pavolini but when Petacci saw her she flew into a jealous rage and stormed at Mussolini. She cursed him and demanded to know why the other woman was there at all. Cucciati defended herself with equal vigour and in the middle of it, Mussolini attempted to pacify them both until, at last, he threw his hands into the air and bellowed at them both to stop.

Petacci's hysteria ended with her falling to the floor, hurting her knee, and she dissolved into tears as Mussolini strode out of the room and sought refuge in the garden. Elena Curti Cucciati, however, still retained her poise and her sense of service. Since there was no news of Pavolini and the troops he had brought as far as Como, she volunteered to return there in an attempt to find out what had happened. She left in the early afternoon, heading with incredible determination back to Como. There, the situation was slowly getting out of hand. In a state of civil war, a bullet answered most questions and very often provided the final answer.

Rachele Mussolini, stranded with her two children in Cernobbio, saw some of the universal terror. Surrounded by panic and horror, she watched fearfully as men were shot in the streets. One man, recognised by the partisans as a Fascist official, was gunned down in front of the building in which Rachele and her frightened children had sought refuge. A group of war-wounded Republican soldiers from a nearby hospital attempted to escape and hobbled through the streets, only to be cut down in the withering fire of partisans seeking revenge against those who had terrorised them, imprisoned them and tortured them in the past.

During the morning of April 26, one of the young Militiamen who still remained on guard over Rachele, told her that there was no chance of her joining Il Duce, since Pavolini had been wounded and was now unable to organise his promised troops. And as all hope ebbed away from her, Rachele tried to comfort her children and shield them as best she could from the nightmare that had overtaken the world outside.

Otto Kisnatt sped through Cernobbio in the early afternoon with the weary troop of SD men who had come with him from Gargnano. He forced the pace along the snaking, unevenly surfaced road that bent perilously round the jagged shoreline of the lake. Where Mussolini and his loosely-knit convoy had trundled, he moved urgently, and arrived in Menaggio at two in the afternoon hot, angry and worried. Again, in Menaggio, there was no sign of the man he was supposed to be guarding. He asked everywhere for news of Mussolini's whereabouts. A soldier pointed disinterestedly towards the hills at the back of the town.

"He went that way," the soldier said. "This morning."

"Where was he going?" Kisnatt demanded.

"Take a look at a map," the soldier replied. "The road leads to Lake Lugarno."

Kisnatt's heart missed a beat. Switzerland! It was the worst he could imagine.

But fate decided that Mussolini never went further towards Switzerland than the Hotel Miravelle in Grandola.

Mussolini had been sent back inside the building by one of Birzer's SS guards and he now busied himself once more with the documents, letters and lists with which he had crammed two briefcases.

As the hours dragged by, Birzer grew increasingly depressed. He was wet, cold, hungry and tired, but his chief fear was that Mussolini might yet make some attempt to reach the Swiss border. It was only twelve kilometres away and he had the feeling, almost the certain feeling, that if Tarchi and Buffarini-Guidi in the other Alfa-Romeos had succeeded in getting across the border, Mussolini and Petacci might be induced to make an effort to follow.

But at about four o'clock in the afternoon came heartening news for the SS man. A dishevelled messenger staggered into the hotel and was seized by a dozen eager hands. Bombarded with a hundred questions, he at last managed to gasp out his message. It was bad news. Buffarini-Guidi and Tarchi had failed. Far from crossing into Switzerland they had been stopped and arrested by Italian border guards. Tarchi had managed to escape but Buffarini-Guidi and a number of his entourage were held prisoner by the border guards who, to a man, had switched their allegiance to the local partisans. It was now clear that refuge in Switzerland was an impossibility. These grim tidings put the assembled Fascist leaders into a further uproar of frantic discussion. Pavolini and his three thousand Blackshirt troops became once more the focal point of their hopes and more attempts were made to contact Como, with the usual lack of success.

It was amid this bedlam that Untersturmfuhrer Birzer was suddenly called in out of the rain to see Mussolini. He found him pacing slowly across the carpet, pale and heavy-eyed but well in control of himself. He began by asking the SS man how many men he had at his disposal and what weapons they had. Warily, Birzer replied that he had twenty-two men of the Waffen-SS, equipped with automatic weapons, heavy machine guns and an anti-tank gun.

Mussolini nodded. "You know the situation, Commendore? Some of my people have been held at the border?" When Birzer said he did, Mussolini continued. "I want you to take every man you have and go to the border and rescue them."

Birzer protested that it was his duty to stay with Il Duce. He refrained from pointing out that Mussolini had twice previously tried to shake him off. Without raising his voice, Mussolini countered that the SS group were under an obligation to help him when he requested aid, and finally, with reluctance, Birzer agreed to make a battle plan for an advance towards the border. But, playing for time, he insisted on being provided with a driver, an Italian who knew the local terrain to which Mussolini agreed. Escorting Birzer to the door Il Duce spoke to a group of men in a passage and they broke into a chorus of excited Italian with accompanying gesticulations before one of their number was pushed sullenly forward. This man prevaricated, saying he wasn't sure of the way to the border. He also indicated that he did not care to go with the Germans. Finally, he said he was hungry and wanted a meal first and Mussolini, in the manner of a man tired of arguing with fractious children, agreed that the rescue attempt should be postponed until the guide had eaten.

Outside the hotel, Birzer went through the motions. He called Guenther to round up the rest of the 2/2 Flak Abteilung and outlined a plan of assault, using light weapons and hand grenades. But as he did so, he sensed a reluctance within the Germans to carry out the assault. He dismissed them to check weapons and spoke to Guenther. The husky Waffen-SS veteran made it clear that he and his men were ready, as ever, to obey orders. But that was not to say they were in favour of risking their lives for Italians. Birzer understood. It was to have a bearing on his actions at a much more crucial moment less than a day later.

Fortunately, perhaps, the rescue operation never materialised. It got lost in the unending confusion within the Hotel Miravelle. The Italian guide never re-appeared and Birzer did not press the point.

It was with much relief that Birzer welcomed the arrival of Kisnatt. He had never trusted nor liked the man, nor indeed any other official of the Sicherheitdienst or the Gestapo. But at least he was another German in authority. In his usual brisk manner, Kisnatt demanded to know what had been happening and Birzer told him briefly of the day's events. Kisnatt muttered a soft curse and strode away into the hotel. There, he saw Mussolini engulfed by a crowd of his fellow countrymen. Mussolini recognised the SD man and, with something of a forced smile, welcomed him into his room. Immediately, Kisnatt began to question him. Why had he broken his promise not to leave Milan. Mussolini parried the questions and brought up the subject of the two Ministers and their capture by the Italian border guards, and then asked Kisnatt if he, too, was prepared to go to the border to bring them back.

"I could go to the border," Kisnatt replied carefully. "But it would not do much good to try to force the Swiss. But tell me, Duce, what business had one of your Ministers near the Swiss border?'

The direct question threw Mussolini off balance temporarily. He stared at the floor for a few moments before lifting his head with a glimmer of the old arrogance.

"I . . . er, I sent them to the border so that they could negotiate with the authorities about my entrance into Switzerland."

"The German authorities," Kisnatt replied with slow emphasis, "are strictly against your entry in Switzerland. Duce, and . . ."

"I know, I know," Mussolini said quickly. "But now the matter has been resolved. We shall continue our journey to Sondrio and Merano, where the German ambassador has settled." Mussolini's manner was that of a recalcitrant boy and he seemed anxious to appease Kisnatt's wounded feelings. To some extent he did so, for Kisnatt, although still suspicious, withdrew and left Mussolini once more immersed in his papers.

Outside, the latest news to hit the untidy band of Fascists was the sudden and unexpected departure of the Minister of Defence, Marshal Graziani, from the entourage. The news came by messenger from Cadenabbia for Graziani had not even thought it worth saying farewell to the man he had served so long and, in his way, so faithfully for years. Graziani and his staff had withdrawn from Menaggio earlier in the day and set up a mobile headquarters in Cadenabbia along with hundreds of others who had straggled along the lake road from Como in the wake of Mussolini. Graziani had followed thus far with increasing reluctance but the disorder, the irresolution, the hopelessness of the whole enterprise finally convinced him that it was a wasted journey. Abruptly, he decided that his proper place was with his army, and he left to join his command. Many others, both officers and soldiers, left with him or drifted away in their own directions with their own plans for seeing out the war as quietly as they could. Leutnant Wilhelm Hurtmanns, the Panzer propaganda officer, was amongst them. Quietly, he slipped off his uniform, changed into civilian clothes and drove back to Milan. Fluent in Italian, he was to assume a new name and a new life amid the upheaval of post-war Italy—and to witness and record the terrible events of those violent, bitter days.

With Buffarini-Guidi gone and Tarchi with him, there was left in the Hotel Miravelle but a shred of Fascist power. As Mussolini had remarked earlier in the day to Elena Curti Cucciati, he would soon be alone. Around him in the hotel was a handful of the most faithful—or the most desperate. This trapped and dwindling flock knew the wolves were prowling but not when they would pounce. Their morale almost at zero, their nerves on edge, they could only wait and wonder what would happen next.

Perhaps the only person in the hotel who was there from choice was Clara Petacci, faithful companion of Mussolini for the past thirteen years. She had met Mussolini in 1932 when she was the wife of an officer in the Italian Air Force. Mussolini had been at the zenith of his power, and the beautiful dark-haired Clara had gladly accepted his advances, shared his bed and surrendered to his insatiable sexual appetite. But there was more to their relationship than sexual exercise, important though that was. Petacci was vain, impulsive, generous and silly. She was far more aware of the latest fashion than of the affairs of state. She was capable of hysteria, given to frequent and lengthy sulks, petulant and jealous. But she was undoubtedly pretty and she knew it. She had shining black hair, dark eyes which she liked to think were green. Her body was exquisitely shaped and her legs long and straight. She had large breasts which moved gently as she walked. Once she had confided to her watchdog, the SS Obersturmfuhrer Franz Spogler that her breasts embarrassed her because they were so large and that she had contemplated an operation to reduce their size, but Mussolini had vetoed the idea declaring lustily that he liked her bust the way it was. Petacci was basically stupid and utterly feminine but she was warm-hearted and kind. When she was happy, she was a girlish chatterbox, but she was often sad and lonely, always suspecting Mussolini of infidelity whenever he was unable to be with her.

Much of her life had been spent just waiting for him. She had a luxurious apartment in the Palazzio Venetia in Rome during the good years when Mussolini ruled Italy from Rome, but she was very often alone amid the splendour and passed the time playing records or reading romantic novels or changing her hairstyle or making up or trying on new dresses, or just lying alone on a couch staring at the ceiling. She was a hypochondriac, often protesting she was ill but recovering quickly when Mussolini appeared at her bedside. In fact, she was only seriously ill once in her life, when after a miscarriage she contracted peritonitis and nearly died. At that time, Mussolini revealed something of his deep attachment to her, insisting on remaining with her during long and anxious hours and even attending an operation she underwent.

For all her faults and idiosyncracies there was no doubt that she loved Mussolini deeply. When she spoke of him in her low, husky, utterly captivating voice, she betrayed her adoration of her unpredictable lover and throughout their long and oft times stormy relationship there was never a suspicion of infidelity on her part. Often, she confessed to Spogler that she had at first been attracted to Mussolini purely because of what he was, the all-powerful Duce. To allow him the favour of her lovely body was, then, merely an adventure, an act that would have obvious reward. But thirteen years later, she was utterly committed and devoted to him, needing him as much as he needed her.

Her influence on him was potentially enormous and it was for this reason that the German overlords of the Republican government had been so careful to keep them together. But in truth she had little interest in politics and rarely attempted to interfere with Mussolini's official life. Clara Petacci's *raison d'être* was simply to be where Mussolini was and it was a dedication that she fulfilled to the last.

The others with whom Mussolini now found himself surrounded in the Hotel Miravelle—with one exception—could hardly be described as intimate friends. Throughout the existence of the Republican government in Gargnano, he had had little to do with the men he had appointed as his Ministers. He preferred to work alone and spent his leisure hours with Clara Petacci or his family, leaving his entourage to their endless bickerings and internecine quarrels. The exception was Niclola Bombacci, a man whom he had known for over forty years and who had been an equally ferocious revolutionary when both were schoolteachers in the town of Gualtieri in 1907. Their personal friendship had survived a political enmity which was provoked when Bombacci chose Communism and Mussolini founded Fascism. But Mussolini had been constant enough in his friendship to see to it that Bombacci did not suffer for his views. Bombacci became one of the few people to whom Mussolini confided his hatred of the German take-over in Italy in 1943, when Mussolini had been held by pro-Allied forces, eventually to be rescued by German paratroops and set up again in a government at Gargnano. Bombacci joined him there, and had remained with him, staunchly loyal.

For the rest, they were a mixture of long-service Fascists and newer appointees who had satisfied their German masters as to their loyalty to the cause. The most impressive of them was Fernando Mezzasoma, the Minister of Popular Culture, whose office was responsible for the permeation of Fascist thought in the country. Mezzasoma, a small nervy individual who wore enormously thick glasses, was a fervent disciple of Fascism and a capable administrator but Mussolini seemed to find his brand of political enthusiasm tiresome. Equally firm in his beliefs was Francesco Barracu, Under-Secretary of the Fascist Council, whose strident voice had been heard throughout the past two days, urging the last stand of Fascism and a glorious end in the Valtellina.

Among the three other Ministers who clung to the wreckage of Fascist power was Paolo Zerbino who had been a minister for only two months, having replaced Buffarini-Guidi at the Ministry of the Interior the previous February. One of Zerbino's tasks prior to taking office had been to co-ordinate the Republican government's efforts to destroy the resistance movement in northern Italy. One of the ironies of his situation was that this attempt, like his later attempts to negotiate with the partisans, had ended in utter failure. On the fringe of this nucleus were two others, Ruggero Romano, Minister of Public Works, and Augusto Liverani, Minister of Communications.

There was a sprinkling of lesser officials—Mussolini's secretary, the energetic, fiercely loyal Luigi Gatti, Paolo Porta, the Fascist chief in Lombardi, and Mussolini's adjutant Colonel Vito Casalinuovo. There were also numerous and varied followers of the Fascist cause, including Alfredo Coppolo, Rector of Bologna University and President of the Institute of Fascist Culture; Ernesto Daquanno, director of the Stefani news agency and chief public relations man to the government; Mario Nudi, President of the Fascist Agricultural Association; and dozens of aides, serving officers and the families of many of those who had come thus far with all they possessed.

Mussolini's son Vittorio was also there with his family, and his nephew Vito and Clara Petacci's brother Marcello, still masquerading as a Spanish diplomat.

The one notable absentee from the gathering which milled endlessly beneath the dripping skies over Grandola, was the man who had promised to save them all, and whose name was continually on their lips—Alessandro Pavolini. Nothing had been heard of him since the morning he had returned to Como swearing to live up to his promise to bring three thousand dedicated soldiers to fight to the death for their leader.

And now their only possible link with him might be a girl on a bicycle pedalling her way frantically to Como.

7

Mussolini had accepted promptly and with gratitude Elena Curti Cucciati's offer to go to Como to trace the missing Pavolini. For fear of being stopped by partisans en route, she chose not to go by car but instead looked around the village of Grandola for a bicycle. The only one she could find was a police bicycle, cumbersome and oversized for her, but she climbed on and pedalled down the winding hill to Menaggio heading for Como. The ride proved an exhausting one for the young girl. Long before reaching Como, she was tired, hot and, to some degree, frightened. In every village, she found the windows of the houses draped with red to indicate sympathy with the partisans. Groups of armed resistance men patrolled the road in several places and although they did not question the girl on the bicycle, she was nevertheless afraid each time she approached them.

As Kisnatt had seen, Como was already in a state of anarchy, and Elena had difficulty locating Pavolini amid the swirling movement of people, partisans, German units, odd knots of Republican soldiery and refugees flowing in from the encroaching war zone. The Prefecture was in turmoil. A new regime had taken control of the building and the previous occupants had fled. In other Fascist strongholds in the town, there was evidence of precipitate flight but at last, in the Fascist Federation building, she caught up with Pavolini. Breathlessly, she ran to him and told him that Mussolini was desperately awaiting him in Menaggio. Pavolini responded by leaping into an armoured vehicle with a crew of six men accompanied by half a dozen others but he refused to take Elena with him. She thus found herself alone in a town which was erupting with the sound of gunfire. But with commendable resolution, she remounted her bicycle and pedalled off in the wake of Pavolini's car back towards Menaggio. After nearly an hour she caught up with him.

It was at Argegno, halfway to Menaggio. Here she found the armoured car, stopped amid a convoy of German lorries. Dishevelled, tired, hungry and anxious, she begged the crew of the armoured car to give her a lift. They took her aboard and she rode with them in the rain towards Menaggio. She had done what she set out to do. She had located Pavolini and the forces he had mustered from all those with which he had boasted he would save his leader.

They were all there with her in the one vehicle!

In Milan, the partisan Liberation Committee had gained almost complete control. The general strike, called for the previous day, was now fully effective and the city had ground to a halt amid outbreaks of unbridled violence. All the key buildings in the city, including the radio station and the Prefecture, had been occupied by partisans whose attempts at government were shattered by continual factional arguments that erupted among the power-thirsty individual groups.

The Committee had occupied the former Republican Territorial Command building, the Plazzo Biera, where General Cadorna—perhaps the only man to come out of this paroxysm with honour—had installed himself and his high command. On the first floor was Cadorna's office and next to it, in what had been the office of the Fascist General Diamonte, was the fiery revolutionary with the characteristically theatrical names of Colonello Valerio. A lifelong Communist, a man of proven bravery in battle during the Spanish Civil War, he nursed a deep hatred of Fascists. A good organiser, a methodical man, he had remained an obscure, shadowy figure in the partisan movement until now. His real name was Walter Audisio, a name as yet unheard of outside the secretive circles of the Committee of Liberation.

But that Thursday afternoon, as he amused himself searching through the drawers and cupboards in the office, confiscating Diamonte's pistol and packets of ammunition left behind in his desk, Audisio was only hours away from an appalling kind of fame.

Pier Bellini's heart pounded with excitement when he drove the old Fiat southward over the bridge, the Ponte del Passo, which linked the two sides of Lake Como beneath the rolling mountains. In all the long months of campaigning against the Germans and the Italian Fascists, he had never won so marvellous a victory. Not only had he bluffed the German garrison in Domaso into complete surrender, he had now used the surrender note signed by the German commander there to induce another Werhmacht garrison—this time at Delebio—to lay down their arms. It was an impressive feat for the leader of a tiny band of twenty-five men. He had defeated more than a hundred well-armed German infantrymen without a shot being fired—all accomplished by the oldest trick in warfare—making the enemy believe they were opposed by an overwhelming force. Bellini had of course been helped by the shattered morale of the German troops who were faced with defeat on the Italian front and aware of the unmistakeable signs of collapse back home in Germany. None the less the men of the 52nd Garibaldi Brigade had every right to the elation which surged through them at that moment.

Accompanied by Urbano Lazzaro his able second-in-command, Hofmann the Swiss and a number of his regular mountain fighters, Bellini was determined to press his good fortune to the limit. He now controlled the northern end of the lake from Domaso to well beyond the most vital crossing point at Ponte del Passo, and was now planning to push his area of command further south, to the villages of Gravedona and Dongo.

Slowly, step by step, Pier Bellini was building a trap into which the biggest prize of all would fall. It was not yet fully prepared and would not be for another twelve hours.

But he was to be given the time, and it would turn out to be a gift from a most improbable quarter.

Untersturmfuhrer Birzer, thoroughly depressed by the miserable situation in which he found himself, never ceased to curse the bad luck that had selected him for this hopeless expedition. He had barely slept for thirty-six hours and during that time had eaten only one hasty meal—and that from a ration tin. The sulky Italian weather matched his mood. He began to think of the Russian front where even though the weather was bitter, there was some purpose, some order, whereas here in Italy there was nothing but chaos. Moodily he stood in the doorway of the Hotel Miravelle and surveyed the grey outlook of a fast-falling dusk. Then his mind strayed homeward to his family and their new home in the Munich suburb of Rosenheim where his wife and sons had moved after their apartment had been wrecked in an American air raid. What was happening in Germany he could only guess, but his guesses gave rise to no particular optimism.

The rest of the men of the 2/2 Flak Abteilung were in no better mood. Even Guenther was showing the signs of strain. The Unterscharfuhrer had given up asking what they were to do next after Birzer had snapped at him that he just didn't know. The SS unit must wait and see, like everyone else. Inside the hotel, the core of Fascist Ministers had temporarily ceased their arguing and waited in edgy silence for the next announcement on the radio. They mentioned Pavolini only occasionally but the hope that once had buoyed them now receded further and further from their minds and their conversation.

Kisnatt expressed to Birzer his contempt for all the Italians and the SS man agreed that they were indeed a worthless bunch. But he was conscious of his duty to guard Mussolini and still determined to obey his orders whether Il Duce liked it or not. But right now, he was sick to death of everything.

It was in this mood that Mussolini's orderly, Carradori, found him a few minutes after five o'clock that Thursday evening. Carradori approached the German and told him that Mussolini wished to speak with him. Birzer nodded, automatically brushed his tunic with his hand, and followed the orderly to the ground-floor reception room where Mussolini had set up his office. He surmised that the reason for this latest interview would be to discuss rescuing the two Ministers held at the border. The Italian who was to lead the SS men had never re-appeared and with darkness almost upon them, Birzer was prepared to argue the impracticability of any such attempt. As it turned out, however, Mussolini never mentioned it. He was standing before a table with his hands on his hips. His eyes looked puffy and tired and he had aged perceptibly. Not only did he look every day of his sixty-one years, but his voice was that of an old, weary man.

"Good evening, Commendore," he said in flat, listless tones. "You will wish to know our plans, I daresay."

"Yes, Duce."

"Well, we are moving north to Merano." He spoke with what Birzer thought was a total lack of interest. "We shall move at once."

Birzer stood stock still before him. Throughout this worrying day, he had waited for some positive order but now, when it came, he felt only anger. Wet, cold and worried, he was in no mood to accept any more commands that day.

"With respect, Duce, I must tell you I am in no position to move immediately," he replied, keeping his voice carefully the right side of insolence. "My men have been on duty almost without a rest for the past thirty-six hours and they have had only one meal. I must insist they be allowed a night's rest."

For a moment, Mussolini frowned with surprise and his mouth opened as though on the point of uttering some angry reply. Then he sighed, peered myopically for a second or two at the maps spread on the table and said in a low voice. "Very well, Commendore, if you wish. We shall delay until five in the morning."

Birzer thanked him for his consideration, Mussolini nodded and the SS officer withdrew. For the very best of reasons, Birzer had won a twelve-hour delay in the timetable of Mussolini's slow progress northward.

It was sheer irony that the one man so devoted to protecting Mussolini's life should be the one to waste his most valuable asset—time. For in that twelve-hour delay, Untersturmfuhrer Fritz Birzer had unwittingly set a time limit on Mussolini's life.

Only eighteen kilometres away, the barrier to all Mussolini's plans for escape and survival was dropping into place. Pier Bellini had succeeded in Dongo as he had succeeded in the other German garrisons. The Italian Muti unit stationed there had fled their posts during the day and the German officer left in charge of a company of dispirited reserve troops willingly laid down his arms after the preliminary ritual of signing a surrender document. Bellini was now master of the whole stretch of the narrow strip of land between the lake and the mountains which dominated the grey water. Now there remained the task of consolidating and issuing arms to the menfolk, mostly old villagers and boys, the only males still left in the communities.

So far, it had been all too easy for the 52nd Garibaldi Brigade. But Bellini was well aware that it still might come to a fight. In that case he would need more than the two dozen partisans who really constituted his mythical siege force. The arms captured from the Germans needed to be carefully distributed and there was a vital need to patrol the roads leading through Dongo to the south and Ponte del Passo to the north. There had to be barricades and guards in prepared positions ready to repel any hostile movement from either direction.

And thus, while Mussolini was agreeing to delay his departure from Menaggio, Pier Bellini set off to put his plans into effect. But neither knew that their actions had already predestined their meeting face to face for the first time in their lives.

The abortive attempt to reach safety in Switzerland had ended in humiliating failure and the only result had been to lower still further the declining morale of those who surrounded Mussolini in the Hotel Miravelle. Birzer observed that the Italians not only showed hostility to him and his men but they were now beginning to quarrel with each other again. Frustration and tension plus the anxiety they all felt, gave way to frequent bouts of ill-tempered argument and it was with evident relief that the bickering Italians heard that they were to make a move at dawn the following morning. Meanwhile they were to leave the gloomy hotel and return to Menaggio for the night.

Before leaving, however, Mussolini again called Birzer into the reception room where he had remained almost continually throughout the day, and this time questioned the SS man closely. He seemed more than usually concerned about the strength of the force which was to protect him on the journey north. To this, Birzer could only reply that he had at his disposal a squad of first-class troops with adequate weapons, plus a number of SD men and a few German police who had attached themselves to the column between Como and Menaggio.

"And do you think these are sufficient for us to travel safely to the north, Commendore?" Mussolini asked.

"I think so," Birzer said.

"Will they be prepared to fight, if necessary?"

"They will do everything necessary to protect you, Duce," Birzer answered guardedly.

"Good." Mussolini's voice was low and he stared at the carpet as if deep in thought. Then he brightened. "Of course, we shall soon be joined by a force of three thousand men. They are on their way from Como . . . they will be with us soon . . ."

Birzer was sceptical about this for he had seen no signs of troops arriving—on the contrary the Italian unit which hitherto had been regarded as Mussolini's escort had vanished during the day along with Marshal Graziani. Birzer's forebodings about the journey northward had been reinforced by Kisnatt who regarded the immediate future with a mixture of despair and defiance. He told Birzer that the situation in Como was one of indescribable chaos. The partisans, he said, were in control of the whole area and added that the column would be extremely lucky if it did not come in contact with them during the following days.

"There's only one way to get out of this," Kisnatt confided. "And that's to shoot anyone who gets in the way. This lot"—he indicated the Italians wandering around the hotel—"are our worst enemies. They'd shoot us if they had the chance—or if they had the nerve."

Birzer answered non-committally. He had no more liking for, nor any more faith in the Italians than did Kisnatt, but felt it futile to dwell on it. He could only agree with the view that Mussolini must have been a remarkable man to have controlled those wayward Italians for nearly a quarter of a century. The more he saw of them, the more remarkable the achievement seemed to be. The tragic plight of the once powerful Mussolini generated a certain sympathy in Birzer, who held no particular brief for Fascism and was not even a convinced Nazi. He was determined to do the best he could for the man. Such were his orders of course, but there was more to it than that. Pity, perhaps. Birzer couldn't really tell.

After a day of futile activity, Mussolini and the remains of his entourage filtered back down the road to Menaggio and prepared to wait out the night before resuming the slow trek north. Birzer and Kisnatt supervised the installation of the Ministers, their families and staff in premises where earlier in the day they had snatched a rest. Mussolini himself elected to stay close to Birzer and withdrew to a room in the schoolhouse barracks.

For the Waffen-SS group a night under the schoolhouse roof which Birzer had won for them was welcome. They had endured a continuous spell of duty in the rain and cold which had begun more than thirty-six hours before. Birzer himself had a headache, his muscles ached and his brain was addled by the unceasing necessity to retain command of a situation which threatened to get out of control at any moment.

No sooner had he stretched himself on the camp bed in a room near the main entrance, than he heard voices outside his door. It was a messenger from Mussolini. Il Duce wanted to see him and once more they discussed the journey, tracing the proposed road north along the side of Lake Como, across the Ponte del Passo and eastward along the fringe of the mountain barrier which separates Italy from the body of Europe. Mussolini again proposed making for Merano, where the German ambassador had set up his headquarters and which was now the titular capital of the crumbling Fascist Republic. And at frequent intervals he spoke of Pavolini and the rescuing army he was to bring to the Valtellina. The discussion, Birzer thought, was fairly pointless, since he could only repeat that he was confident the journey could be safely made with the forces at his disposal. Mussolini was apparently satisfied with the plans for the morning and Birzer returned to his camp bed. This time he managed to drift into a shallow sleep. It was after midnight when he was awakened by a knocking on the door. One of his SS men was on the threshold.

"Herr Untersturmfuhrer," stammered the excited soldier, "there is another of our units here. They have just arrived in the town . . . several hundred men and a long convoy of trucks."

It was the best news Birzer could have wished for. "Who are they?" he demanded.

"I think they're Luftwaffe, sir," said the soldier. "But I have brought the officer to see you. He's outside."

"Bring him in. What's his name?"

"Fallmeyer, sir. Oberleutnant Fallmeyer."

Quickly, Birzer slipped out of the bed and reached for his tunic. He had it half on when the door opened and an officer in the pale blue uniform of the Luftwaffe entered the room. He was tall and slender, with a tanned face and brown eyes. Birzer noted the colour of his collar tabs, since the various hues denoted different units. Yellow, for instance, was worn by aircrew. Fallmeyer's was brown—communications.

Birzer held out his hand, observing as he did so that the Luftwaffe man was smartly turned out. And when he spoke, Birzer recognised a South German accent similar to his own.

"I'm Fallmeyer," the other man said crisply. "Glad to see you."

"Birzer. Waffen-SS. I am very pleased to see you. Where are you making for?"

Fallmeyer shrugged. "Northward, of course. Towards Austria."

The two Germans talked for some ten minutes, during which time, Birzer discovered that Fallmeyer and his men—some 160 of them in thirty or more trucks—had retreated from the south and had been on the move for some days. Fallmeyer mentioned that his convoy had been held up a number of times during the previous day by partisan units, who had allowed them to proceed—since the convoy consisted only of Germans leaving Italy to return to Germany.

"They didn't appear very interested in us," Fallmayer said. "I think they were really looking for Italians."

Birzer's heart sank. "Italians," he echoed gloomily. "I am surrounded by them." He hesitated for a moment or two and then continued. "There is one in particular who would be, shall we say, most interesting to any partisans we met..."

Fallmeyer nodded. "So I understand."

"It's Mussolini, of course," Birzer said.

"Yes, everyone in Menaggio seems to know he's here."

Birzer snorted. "Of course! I'm surprised the whole world doesn't know. We've been here all day and they've been running all over the countryside. Hopeless."

They lapsed into silence. The arrival of the Luftwaffe convoy was a godsend to Birzer, but if the presence of this relatively powerful force was to be of real use to him, he must have the confidence and co-operation of Fallmeyer. He weighed the man up before putting the question he so wanted to ask. At last, he spoke.

"What would you say if I suggested that we merge our units and move north together? We'd all be safer that way, I think."

"Certainly," Fallmeyer replied, "anything you say... but there is one thing."

"What is it?"

"I don't really want to know anything about . . . well, Mussolini. I want to get my men and myself back home with the minimum of trouble. You understand me?"

"I understand. I shall be responsible for him."

For a few minutes more, the two Germans discussed the formation of the combined convoy. Fallmeyer had drawn up his trucks on the loop road through Menaggio which ran alongside the lake. It was agreed that the Italians, led by Birzer, would proceed first, with Fallmeyer and the Luftwaffe unit about three hundred metres behind. A Luftwaffe motor cyclist would maintain contact between the two sections of the convoy. When these details had been arranged Fallmeyer withdrew, leaving a slightly more hopeful Birzer alone with his thoughts.

Elena Curti Cucciati crouched on the floor of the big armoured car as it trundled in darkness into Menaggio. On board with her were about a dozen men, including the crew and Alessandro Pavolini. A pitiful group representing the brave battalions for whom Mussolini and his followers had waited in vain. Peering out from the armoured window, Elena saw a scene of utter confusion. Lorries and cars were parked everywhere. Men in a variety of different uniforms and stolid-faced villagers stood by the roadside staring at the comings and goings which had turned their community into a circus since dawn the previous morning. As the armoured car stopped outside the schoolhouse barracks a group of men clustered around the vehicle, shouting in the darkness, for those inside to identify themselves. They fell suddenly silent when the door flew open and Pavolini appeared. He seemed undaunted by the failure of his mission and stepping from the armoured car he raised his fist as if in triumph. He was immediately engulfed by the crowd in the roadway, clamouring for answers to their questions and oblivious of the pouring rain. He pushed his way imperiously through them and entered the building where inside the school door, he met Mussolini. Pavolini again raised his fist in the traditional Fascist salute and the two men faced each other.

"Where are the Blackshirts?" Mussolini's voice sounded sharp with the urgency of the question. Pavolini hesitated and half-turned towards the door, making a limp gesture with his hand, indicating they were outside.

"How many?" Mussolini demanded.

"Twelve."

For a moment, there was total stunned silence. Then Mussolini turned abruptly and walked back to his room, leaving Pavolini white-faced and motionless. The light glistened on the raindrops peppering his black uniform and it illuminated the haggard faces of those who had waited for so long—for nothing.

Slowly, their stupor gave way to curiosity and a barrage of questions bombarded the shaken Pavolini and he answered sullenly, still watching the door through which his leader had marched in a gesture of angry despair. At last the true import of Pavolini's confession began to dawn on them all. There was no army of loyal Blackshirts. There would be no last heroic stand in the Valtellina. The large and well-equipped force which had mustered earlier in the day in Como had lost its stomach for a fight and had surrendered to the Como partisans. There was no help coming. They were alone. Thus, at one o'clock in the morning of Friday, April 27, the hope of a last stand by the fugitive Fascist hierarchy was extinguished.

The profound effect upon Mussolini of this bitter disappointment was evident an hour later when he sent for Otto Kisnatt. The guard told him that Mussolini had not slept at all and that he had been talking with a stream of visitors ever since he had returned from Grandola. Kisnatt saw all the signs of utter fatigue in the face of the doomed leader. His appearance was unusually untidy although he still wore the uniform of the militia. When he spoke his voice was low.

"Pavolini has arrived," he began, "but where are the ten armoured cars and the men? Nowhere! Two old armoured cars are all we have." He paused. "This is a catastrophe. Nevertheless I still intend to leave at five and we shall try to reach Merano within the day."

"It would do you good to try to get some sleep," Kisnatt replied sympathetically. "The last two days have been very strenuous for you, Duce."

Mussolini smiled wearily. "You are right, Commendore." He walked heavily across to one of the windows and stared out into the black, wet night, seeing nothing.

"I have a foreboding," he said at last. "A very bad one. . . . God knows what is in store for us."

Kisnatt tried to comfort him. "Everything will turn out all right, Duce. But you must get some sleep now."

Mussolini nodded absently and covered his eyes with his hand. Then he let his arm drop to his side and continued to stare out of the window as Kisnatt withdrew from the room.

Soon after this, it was Birzer's turn. Mussolini questioned him once more about the state of his troops and their armament and Birzer once more reassured him, adding that they were now able to travel in company with Fallmeyer's large force of Luftwaffe troops. Mussolini, however, was unmoved by this news and made no comment other than a weary gesture of acceptance. Birzer's impression was that he was past caring. He appeared to have withered visibly inside his uniform. His movements dragged.

It was after four in the morning when the SS man left him. To Kisnatt Mussolini had confessed that only God knew what was in store for them. To Birzer he conveyed the impression that he didn't really care any more. And it was an impression which was to linger to the end. From this moment, Mussolini took practically no decision, nor any real interest, in his fate. From this moment, he was content to be merely at the mercy of events.

Like Mussolini, Pier Bellini delle Stelle had no sleep that night, but he had no sense of fatigue after all the excitement of the day. Having gained control of the lakeside, Bellini and his second-in-command, Urbano Lazzaro, had set about augmenting their forces, handing out arms and instructions to the men of the lake villages who welcomed the 52nd Garibaldi Brigade as liberators. By midnight, Bellini had the makings of an organised force which numerically bore some relation to the area he held. It was not a very prepossessing army, however, for apart from the younger partisans, it consisted mainly of old men and boys outside the age limits for conscription or war work. None the less, he had established a chain of command from Dongo to beyond the Ponte del Passo and held all the surrendered Germans under armed guard in Germasino.

In the early hours of Friday, April 27, he set out on a final tour of inspection, visiting partisan commands in Delebio, the guard on the Ponte del Passo, the groups in Domaso, the guarded Germans in Gravedona and, consulted with a unit of Italian customs guards at Germasino which, under Sergeant Giorgio Buffelli, an intelligent and resourceful man, had decided to work with the partisans. Bellini and Buffelli had known each other for some time, having collaborated clandestinely in harassing the Germans. Finally, at about four in the morning, Bellini returned to Dongo where he had set up his headquarters in the municipal building, and held a consultation with his principal lieutenants. With him were Lazzaro, the Swiss Hofmann, the leader of the partisans in Musso—a village a few hundred metres south of Dongo—named Davide Barbiere, and Buffelli. It was decided that Barbiere, a veteran anti-Fascist, and two of his men would stand guard through the dawn on a roadblock which would be placed across the Musso-Dongo road at a point where a towering granite rock bulged out from the mountain to the very edge of the lake. The road at this point cut into the rock like a step. Above the road was sheer rock: below it, the lake. It was an ideal place for an ambush. Indeed, it had been notorious in an earlier age, when bandits roamed the mountains and frequently held up the carriages of those foolish enough to venture along this road.

While Mussolini was pacing the floor of his room in Menaggio, Bellini walked up the slight incline of the road out of Dongo to make a last check on the roadblock. Two men were guarding it. Another waited further down the road and two more partisans had set up a machine gun post above Dongo. Only then, when he was quite satisfied that it was reasonable to do so, did Bellini accept the offer of a bed from Hofmann. At four-thirty, he drove back to Domaso in the Fiat with Hofmann and Urbano Lazzaro and the three men fell fast asleep in the Hofmann villa.

It was pitch dark, cold and wet. A thin fog drifted up from the lake and the raindrops dripped off the bare trees as Otto Kisnatt stood smoking by the side of his car outside the school, while those inside made frantic preparations to continue the journey. Kisnatt thrust his hands in his coat pockets to warm them and felt the brochure about Lake Como which one of his men had given him the previous evening. He examined it by torch-light and came across a quotation from the composer Franz Liszt, written in 1838.

"I do not know," it read, "any part of the country which is blessed more than the shores of Lake Como—made to inspire the story of two happy lovers.'"

Kisnatt smiled grimly. A hundred odd years ago, it may have been true. But now? He screwed the brochure into a ball and threw it away—a gesture symbolic of the miserable climax which seemed to be impending on the shores of Como.

Fritz Birzer had been up and about since 4.45, attempting to put some kind of order into the confusion that reigned all about him. The remnants of Fascist power scampered like frightened children. Some begged Birzer for petrol or tried to buy it from the SS men with cigarettes and money, first wheedling then cursing the Germans as traitors. Only one—a woman—aroused any sympathy. She was a German, the wife of an Italian official. Her husband, she said, had vanished in the night, leaving her with their child and a car without fuel. Birzer ordered that she be given a tankful of the precious petrol and promised to take care of her and the child. But he never saw them again.

Two civilians each carrying a suitcase approached Kisnatt at that moment. He thought he recognised them as two of Mussolini's Ministers.

"We have two valuable suitcases here," one of them said in bad German.

"We would like you to take them with you and guard them for us," said the other.

Kisnatt replied that he had no room in his car, and suggested they put their luggage on the lorry carrying the SS men and their equipment—a plan to which Birzer agreed. Much later, when it was too late to matter, Birzer saw the contents, but now he was concerned only with getting the convoy under way and joined to the Luftwaffe unit waiting to move off from the loop road by the lake.

Shortly after five, Mussolini strode out of the school and made his way to the green Alfa, which was parked behind the big armoured vehicle. He paused for a moment to peer around in the gloom. Then, he issued the last order he was ever to utter.

"We shall now leave for Merano."

8

It was just getting light when the fisherman Aldo Castelli set out from his home in Domaso to walk to the former German barracks in Gravedona where the Germans were being guarded by partisans. It had been a strenuous night for him, as it was for the rest of Bellini's men, and Castelli managed to snatch a little sleep before facing a new day. One thought was uppermost in Castelli's mind as he strode along the empty road between the two villages. The day before, he had noticed piles of clothing in the stores of the German garrison, among them a number of big, heavy Wehrmacht overcoats. Castelli coveted these as he remembered the long cold nights which he had spent in the mountains. Here was a golden opportunity to win a warm overcoat, something dear to the heart of the cheery fisherman. With a Belgian automatic machine gun slung over his shoulder, baggy trousers and an old coat, Castelli cut an amusing figure as he whistled softly and walked jauntily along the lakeside.

Suddenly, through the early morning mist, he perceived the figure of another man walking towards him. Whipping the gun into his hands, he advanced cautiously. The man was unarmed and was carrying a suitcase. At about ten metres from each other, they both stopped.

"Where are you going? Who are you?" Castelli demanded, his finger on the trigger of the gun.

"It's all right," the other man replied. "Don't shoot. I live here." He went on to explain that he had travelled overnight from Milan and had caught a boat from Lecco on the other side of the lake to a landing point a little north of Menaggio and had been walking for an hour towards his home. The two talked for a few minutes, during which Castelli heard the latest news from Milan and explained to the stranger how the partisans of Domaso had taken control of the district. And then, quite casually, the man told Castelli something that shook him visibly.

"There's a big convoy heading this way," he confided. "I saw them from the lake. Hundreds of lorries are leaving Menaggio and going towards Dongo."

"Lorries? Who do you think is in them. Tedesci?"

"Must be," the other man replied. "Lots of them."

Castelli did not stay for anything more. The vision of his precious overcoat faded as he ran towards the Gravedona barracks. There, without stopping to ask questions, he snatched a bicycle which had been dropped in the courtyard, leapt on it, and pedalled as hard as his strong legs would go, towards Dongo. The town was still deserted as he sped across the open square and pounded up the hill towards the Vall'Orba, the big rock where the roadblock had been set up. A few dozen metres short of the rock, he found a partisan standing in the road. He recognised the man as a resident of Gravedona named Frangi Bellati, who had volunteered to join the partisans of the Luigi Clerici Brigade the previous day. Castelli threw down his bicycle and ran breathlessly to the astonished Bellati.

"Have they seen anything at the roadblock?'" he gasped.

Bellati shrugged. "Nothing. It's as quiet as the grave."

"Well, it won't be for long," Castelli panted. "There's a damned great convoy of tedesci coming this way."

An unhappy-looking German Luftwaffe police motorcyclist sat astride the saddle of his combination machine and watched unemotionally as the stream of vehicles passed him. First there came a big armoured car, more like a lorry with armour plating, with big wheels and a heavy machine gun mounted on the top. It contained Pavolini, the Minister Barracu, Mussolini's adjutant

Colonel Vito Casalinuovo, Nicola Bombacci, a young Air Force officer named Pietro Salustri, a Blackshirt officer, Idreno Utimperghe, Mussolini's orderly Carradori, still holding on to his chief's two briefcases, and Elena Curti Cucciati.

Behind the armoured vehicle came one of the Alfa-Romeos, driven by Mussolini himself. Birzer in his Kubelwagen came next, followed by Kisnatt's car, the Waffen-SS truck and a string of other cars and lorries. In one of them, still masquerading behind Spanish diplomatic plates, sat Marcello Petacci and his sister Clara.

When they had all passed, the Luftwaffe policeman raised his hand to signal the column of Luftwaffe trucks, laden with 160 men and loads of signal gear. As they nosed up the lakeside road and turned northward on to the main highway, the German nodded to his companion in the sidecar, kick-started the motor and gained slowly on the tail of the Italian vehicles.

It was nearly five-thirty.

The procession made slow progress through the tiny villages straddling the road, since the armoured car at its head was forced to take the narrow, rutted road between the houses at little more than walking pace. At Acquaseria, the column stopped. A few villagers were in the streets to watch the vehicles pass and to a small knot of people, Mussolini spoke a few words. He had got out of the Alfa and stood at the roadside, hands on hips in his favourite stance. Behind him, Fritz Birzer watched with interest, unable to see the reason for the stoppage. Then he saw Mussolini walk forward to the armoured car. The door opened, Mussolini climbed in and the column rolled lazily forward once more.

Through Rezzonico, Cremia, Calozzo and Lovezzano, the long line of vehicles passed without incident, the drivers coaxing the vehicles forward in low gear. There was no sign of partisans. Hunched in the Kubelwagen Birzer peered over the collar of his greatcoat and riveted his eyes on the armoured car, taking only an occasional glance at the placid lake to his right.

They came to Musso, and Birzer smiled to himself at the coincidence of the names. He began musing on the possibility of fate linking the two.

The leading vehicles of the column were now nosing up the slight incline on the muddy road out of Musso heading for the Vall'Orba rock when suddenly the armoured car braked to a dead stop. Birzer, in the Kubelwagen, had barely taken in the fact when a single shot from a rifle echoed from the rocky mountains and was followed almost at once by a short burst of machine gun fire. The sounds sawing through the misty air jerked him into action and he tumbled from the vehicle with his own gun at the alert. More firing came from the armoured car and answering shots whistled across the lake. The Waffen-SS men scattered from their trucks and slithered down the shallow embankment to the water's edge, but before they had a chance to join in the action, it was over. The firing stopped abruptly and Birzer noticed the barrier across the road ahead of the armoured car. It had been erected in front of the point where the road swept round a towering rock. Three armed men stood up uncertainly behind the barrier, which seemed to consist of rocks and lumps of timber strewn haphazardly across the carriageway. The armoured car had swerved into the side of the road and two of its huge tyres were flat. Cautiously Birzer crept towards the head of the convoy keeping the armoured car between him and the line of fire from the men at the barricade. Glancing back down the convoy of vehicles which choked the road through Musso, he knew there was no hope of turning back. They were trapped between the narrow street in Musso and the strategically placed rock ahead. A regiment of Panzers would have been no better off, Birzer thought. He yelled to one of his men to fetch Leutnant Fallmeyer and warned the rest to stay alert but not to open fire unless the partisans fired first. Then, crouching by the rear of the armoured car, he waited.

Davide Barbieri could hardly believe his eyes when he first saw the big armoured vehicle lumbering towards him up the incline from Musso. At first, he thought it was on a lone patrol but as the stream of other vehicles came into view he realised it was the van of a large force. One of the two men with him shouted in alarm as the armoured car headed for them, but Barbieri, leader of the Musso community and a veteran partisan, harshly ordered him to shut up and concentrate on aiming at the wheels of the slow-moving vehicle as it came within range of their weapons. Nervously, he squinted down the barrel of his rifle, seeing only the turning tyres and trying not to think about the machine gun which pointed straight down the road towards the flimsy barricade. Then the wheels stopped. The vehicle was about a hundred metres away when Barbieri fired the first shot. The others around him were a second late in opening fire and before they got into action, Barbieri heard the heavy machine gun in the mountain above hammer out a burst. Barbieri pumped more shots at the armoured car, which promptly replied with a hail of fire. A partisan behind the barricade was hit. A cloud of exhaust smoke belched forth from the armoured car as it started up again but it had moved only a metre or two forward when it stopped, its flat tyres causing it to swerve to the side of the road. There was a pause in the firing and a few men scampered from the vehicles immediately behind the armoured car but nothing else happened, and Barbieri peeped carefully over the rocks to take stock of the situation. Quickly, the partisan took out a handkerchief and tied it to a strap of his rifle and poked it into the air. There was no response, so he rose to his feet, his eyes fixed on the machine gun in the turret on top of the leading vehicle. His companions joined him and the three of them stood, waiting beneath the improvised white flag.

Further back on the road to Dongo, Aldo Castelli and Frango Bellati got up from the side of the road where they had thrown themselves when the firing started. Guns in hand, they walked slowly round the massive headland and got a clear view of the halted convoy. The man from Milan had not underestimated the size of the convoy which he had seen leaving Menaggio. As far back as Castelli could see, there was a long line of trucks which reached through Musso and beyond.

Against this enormous force there were but five partisans and a few more manning machine guns in the high rocks above. No one else was about, and Castelli wondered if the men on the machine guns realised the seriousness of the situation. He was sure that one of the gunners had been firing into the lake out of sheer *joie de vivre*, thinking that all the firing had come from his friends on the ground celebrating the end of the war. The fisherman wasted only a few seconds summing up the position, then ran back down the road, grabbed his bicycle and sped into Dongo. The little town was deserted. All the people who the day before had so readily accepted weapons from the partisans now seemed to have vanished, and Castelli was furious.

"Come out!" he yelled. "We need help!" But his voice echoed futilely over the town square. Angrily, Castelli ran to the war memorial standing in the centre of the square, in front of the town hall, and climbed on to the plinth, where the inscription paid tribute to the heroes of an earlier war.

"Cowards!" he roared. "You call yourself Italians and patriots! Show yourselves! You've got guns, come out and use them, or give them to men who will!"

There, on the war memorial the rugged little partisan berated and cursed his fellow countrymen. At last, one or two dragged their feet into the square. Others followed, and Castelli commanded them to bring more logs, rocks and barbed wire up the Musso road to reinforce the barricade. There seemed to be no more firing from the roadblock and Castelli thought it best to get Pier Bellini back to Dongo to take command of the situation there. Once more he pedalled desperately along the road to Domaso and hurried to the Hofmann villa. He burst in on Bellini, who was sleeping heavily, and shook him.

"Pedro," he called, using Bellini's battle name as always. "There are hundreds of tedeschi held up at Dongo. For God's sake come quickly. Hurry!"

Within minutes, Bellini was out of the house, followed by Urbano Lazzaro and Hofmann. Together with Castelli, they climbed into the old Fiat and headed back to Dongo.

Pier Bellini's plans had certainly taken account of the possibility that German troops would try to use the lake road but if, as Castelli reported, they had actually arrived in overwhelming numbers, the outlook for the depleted 52nd Garibaldi Brigade and the villagers who had now joined them, was desperate. He listened for further sounds of battle as he drove furiously through Dongo to the Vall'Orba. There, he stopped the car and walked along the road to where it bent sharply round the protruding rock. At the apex of the bend, he saw the roadblock and the stationary column of vehicles. There was a small party of men standing at the barricade.

Keeping his Sten gun balanced over the crook of his left arm, Bellini tugged at his beard, straightened his cap and walked towards them. The Germans, or whoever were in the convoy, appeared to be as interested in talking as in fighting and Bellini was certain that, once again, his trump card was the element of uncertainty in every man when faced with the unknown. He must therefore keep up the pretence of overwhelming strength, and play for time.

He walked on, approached the barricade, and stopped before two German officers, a civilian and a group of armed soldiers and prayed there was not too many of them.

Alois Hofmann came to stand by his side, ready to translate.

"Tell them," Bellini instructed the Swiss, "that they are heavily outnumbered, but that we wish to avoid unnecessary bloodshed."

Hofmann conveyed the message in German. One of the Germans, who seemed to be the commander of the column, replied in a mixture of German and halting Italian, and said his concern was to merely get out of Italy and return to Germany, via Merano, but warned that he too had a large unit of well-armed men.

Bellini noted the veiled threat in these words. It was necessary now to pull the big bluff. Waving his arms towards the hills, Bellini rattled off fictitious numbers of men and imaginary units, pointed a hand towards the German column and uttered one of the few words of German he had learned.

"Kaputt!"

119

The German withdrew a few paces to speak to the other officer, who had stood a little apart, staring impassively at Bellini throughout the conversation. With a great effort to be casual, Bellini called Castelli and spoke in a low voice.

"Get back to Dongo. Take a couple of men with you and get everyone you can out on to the streets. Put everyone with a gun on the road and send others up into the hills. Tell them to wear colourful shirts, red handkerchiefs round their necks—anything to make them conspicuous. I want the Germans to think there are hundreds of us. Then get to the Ponte del Passo and be ready to blow it up. Don't do any more until you hear from me—but turn out everyone along the road. And make it look really big."

It was a long shot—a gamble. In the past twenty-four hours, Bellini had played against similar odds and won. Now, his life and those of many others dependent on him were at stake in the biggest bluff of all.

On the other side of the barrier, Fritz Birzer eyed the partisans with mixed feelings. This bearded partisan with the peaked cap and a red star on it, was clearly the leader and appeared to be well in control of the situation. He could see perhaps a dozen men, all with modern weapons and there must be more in the mountains above the big rock ahead of them. And around the other side of the rock? Probably dozens more. There was no possibility of the whole convoy turning round, even if the partisans agreed—and there seemed little point in trying to force a way forward. There was no room for manoeuvre and the enemy had the advantage of the heights above the road. Birzer had only twenty-two men he could count on to fight and, above all, he must still protect Mussolini.

It was better to try to negotiate in the hope the partisans would allow them through. The first partisan they had spoken to—it had been Barbieri—had hinted that the Germans—but only Germans—would be allowed to continue. Fallmeyer, who had joined Birzer at the head of the column soon after it stopped, had also gathered as much during a halting conversation with the men at the roadblock. But his talk had not got far—partly because of language difficulties and partly because the men on the other side were reluctant to say too much until their commander arrived. Meantime, Kisnatt had displayed an irritating belligerence and kept demanding that Birzer and his Waffen-SS blast their way through the roadblock. As patiently as he could, Birzer pointed out the futility of fighting when it might be possible to talk their way out—and this assessment was proving accurate.

"They say they've got the place under their control," Fallmeyer reported after talking to the bearded partisan, with the help of a small man with fair hair and blue eyes, who spoke both Italian and German.

"They say they want to avoid bloodshed," the Luftwaffe man went on. "I think they might just let us through. They seem better organised and led than others I've met in the past couple of days, so I think there's a chance."

Birzer nodded. "Good. Do anything they ask, but don't breathe a word about . . . our friend."

"No, naturally." Fallmeyer stepped back to the barricade and spoke again with the bearded man. Birzer caught the words "Deutches Soldaten" and "Luftwaffe" and "Merano" but it was some minutes before Fallmeyer returned. Birzer, looking at his watch, was surprised to find it was eight forty-five.

During his discussions, Fallmeyer said, he had been told that in order to come to an agreement, he must accompany the bearded partisan to his superior partisan commander in Morbegno.

"He says I have to go with him. I think it's the only thing to do. Their leader, the one with the beard, says there will be a truce until I get back. He guarantees my safety."

"And what is it you are going to discuss?" Birzer asked.

"Whether or not we can proceed. I gather they're willing to let only Germans through, but that has still to be approved by some other leader. But in any case, I doubt whether they will let the Italians go."

"I'm sure they won't," Birzer agreed.

"At least, if I go with them, I might be able to see something of their positions. It's our best chance." Fallmeyer walked away towards his scout car, where he told his driver to proceed to the roadblock. The partisans pulled aside the rocks and tree trunks for the Luftwaffe car to move forward. The bearded partisan got in, followed by the interpreter and two others, both armed. It was just after nine o'clock as the car skirted the road around the great rock and disappeared from Birzer's view.

The convoy by this time had spilled most of the passengers as word of the ambush filtered slowly back down the line. Yuone Fancelli was standing by a chipped enamel sign with the word "Musso" on it, talking with some other Italian soldiers, when the news came. By the time it reached the back of the convoy, it had been magnified. There had been a battle! Many had been killed! Mussolini had been captured and hundreds of partisans were coming! One or two truck drivers attempted to turn in the road, but found it impossible, but many—like Fancelli himself—were soon to walk away from it all.

During the discussions at the roadblock, the disabled armoured car had stood lifeless and silent. Inside, Mussolini had remained curiously passive throughout the affair. Immediately the firing had ended and the talking began, he took no further interest in the outside world. He busied himself sorting through, marking and notating the papers in his briefcases, saying little to anyone in the vehicle, which was large enough for several people to sit comfortably. As the parleying at the roadblock continued, a group of anxious men gathered around. The car became a kind of armoured confessional as they shouted through the steel-shuttered windows and spoke in quick, hushed tones at the door.

Untersturmfuhrer Birzer was one of this group and he reported to Mussolini that Fallmeyer had gone with the partisans to arrange for their safe conduct through to Merano. Mussolini, leafing through a pad of papers on his lap, barely looked up. He simply sighed, as though the dramatic events of the day were of no importance to him—or outside his control in any case.

Then another strange incident happened. The rear door of the vehicle opened and Elena Curti Cucciati, who was crouched inside, saw a small figure in overalls peering into the car. She watched, intrigued, as the little figure climbed inside, crawled across to where Mussolini sat and squatted on a seat next to the side door. Elena caught no glimpse of the face, which was partially hidden beneath a helmet but when the helmet was removed a moment later, she recognised the dark curly hair of a woman. It was Clara Petacci, who once again was where she ever wanted to be—beside the man she adored.

On the fringes of Musso, an enterprising village woman was doing a roaring trade selling wine from casks on a barrow, amassing a large stock of cigarettes which she took in payment from the Germans and Italians. But Birzer was in no mood for drinking. Already, while he waited for Fallmeyer, his mind was turning to another alternative. Lake Como at that point is about one thousand metres wide and to cross it in a small boat would not be difficult. The danger, Birzer reasoned, would come from the partisan machine gunners on the big rock overlooking the lake. But it seemed to be a risk worth taking if he could persuade Mussolini to accept it.

Telling the reliable Guenther to keep a strict watch over the armoured car and to fire in the air at the first sign of movement, Birzer, accompanied by his driver Schultze, walked back into Musso to look for some kind of boat on the lakeside. As they walked the length of the convoy, it was obvious to the two men that the Italian group had little faith in a successful outcome of the negotiations with the partisans. Some of the Ministers and ranking officials in the party had already left their cars and, taking such luggage as they could carry, had sought refuge in the village. A steady stream of lesser individuals were walking away from Musso, southwards towards Menaggio and Como. Drawn up close behind the Italian vehicles, the Luftwaffe convoy remained relatively orderly. Truck drivers were in the cabs of their vehicles while the airmen clustered around, talking, smoking or staring across the misty lake. Many of the trucks were loaded with communications equipment but some were fitted with benches for

carrying troops. Birzer took a look inside one. It was a covered
lorry with wooden sides and a canvas top. There were benches
placed on each side and others running crosswise towards the
front of the truck near the driving cab. Littered about the interior
were items of kit, spare tarpaulins and other paraphernalia. Furthermore, the interior was dim and it struck the SS man that
anyone hiding inside the truck would not be easily discovered.

As Leutnant Fallmeyer's car pulled round the Vall'Orba and
rolled down towards Dongo, Pier Bellini silently prayed that
Aldo Castelli had done his work well enough to muster a formid-
able-looking force of partisans in and around the town. Bellini felt
sure that the man sitting next to him was anxious to avoid a fight,
but it was still vital that when he returned to his convoy, he
should impart the information that the partisans had an overwhelming superiority in numbers.

To be sure, Castelli had carried out his task brilliantly.
Dongo, when the German car reached it, was alive with activity.
Bellini recognised some of his men standing at the roadside with
automatic weapons cradled in their arms. Others, whom he did
not know had climbed to the top of the roofs and shouted down
into the street as Bellini ordered the German driver to stop.
Impressively, the partisan leader stepped from the car, had a
few words with one of the men and took the opportunity to wave
an ostentatious arm towards the hills.

"The 52nd Garibaldi Brigade, one of the best units in the area,
are in complete control of the town," Bellini proudly announced
as he re-entered the car. Hofmann translated and advised Fallmeyer to instruct the driver to go slowly. "These partisans
are inclined to shoot at anything German and ask questions
afterwards," he added significantly.

Fallmeyer nodded gravely and leaned forward to relay the
instruction to the driver.

They made slow progress northward and in each village, Bellini stopped to speak to the armed partisans, repeating the same

impressive pantomime as in Dongo. Each time, he invented a fictitious brigade number which was passed on to the subdued Fallmeyer. Through Gravedona, Domaso, Gera Lario and Sorico they were greeted by groups of armed men. while others waved conspicuously from the nearby hillsides. Throughout the area there was an unmistakable impression of armed strength and organisation which wildly exceeded Bellini's greatest hopes and which undoubtedly made an impact on the German commander.

When the car reached Ponte del Passo, Bellini urged even greater caution, telling the German that the bridge was heavily mined. The driver coaxed the car along at walking pace and at the edge of the bridge, Bellini ordered him to stop. He once more descended for a word with the partisans who this time included Castelli. But here, Bellini's smooth-running plans received a nasty jolt. One of the local partisans known only to Bellini by his battle-name "John" took the bearded commander by the arm walked him out of earshot of the German car.

He had disturbing news. It concerned the Garibaldi unit which had attempted to take control of the town of Chiavenna, twenty-five kilometres north of Ponte del Passo, on the road north to Switzerland. There the partisans, under the command of a friend of Bellini's named Dionisio Gambarutti, were engaged in heavy fighting with the German garrison and were calling for reinforcements.

Rapidly, Bellini ticked off in his mind the effects of the information. It was discomforting to know that there were German troops in the area who were still willing and able to hit back in strength. But it was all the more essential to take Fallmeyer back to Dongo as quickly as possible while he was convinced of the partisan advantage in numbers. As to the problem of helping Gambarutti, this was almost out of the question, but he resolved to go to Chiavenna and see for himself.

Again, Bellini gambled. He ordered the Germans to drive across the bridge and take the road to Delebio, where, earlier, the German garrison had surrendered to him. The troops there must be considered disarmed prisoners and Bellini—with considerable psychological insight—banked on the avidity of the garrison commander to defend his action if confronted by another German officer. Accordingly, he drove to the barracks and brought the commander face to face with Fallmeyer.

Addressing the infantry officer he declared. "I have explained to this German officer," indicating Fallmeyer, "that you have wisely surrendered to a superior force of partisan troops who are in control of this area. Will you please be good enough to confirm this to him?"

The infantryman was clearly embarrassed but, in his own defence, told Fallmeyer that his garrison had been surprised and surrounded and that he had had no option but to order his men to lay down their arms in order to avoid unnecessary bloodshed. Bellini was unable to follow the two Germans but, even without Hofmann's help, it was clear from Fallmeyer's face and shrugs of resignation that he realised the position to be a hopeless one.

It was an almost unbelievable triumph and Bellini felt sure now that Fallmeyer would accept any conditions in return for safe passage through partisan territory. And the conditions uppermost in Bellini's mind were simply that if the German element of the Dongo convoy be allowed through, the Italians must be dealt with by the partisans. He was quite certain also that the only objective in the minds of the Germans was to get out of Italy as fast as they could. If there was to be a last-ditch stand at Dongo, it would be the Italians who might make it, but as long as the Germans and Italians remained together, there was a danger the Germans could be dragged into a fight not of their own choosing. Separating them was therefore of prime importance.

There was however, the situation in Chiavenna, and that had to be investigated. Leaving Fallmeyer and his fellow German under armed guard, Bellini borrowed a car, drove back almost to Ponto del Passo but then turned north along the road which, in better days, took tourist traffic from Italy to the ski slopes of St. Moritz via the Splugen Pass.

A few kilometres short of Chiavenna there was an almost continuous sound of firing and the smell of cordite was acrid in the air. With great care, Bellini skirted the core of the battle and amid the bark of machine guns and the whine of bullets he ran zig-zag through the streets. At last he located Gambarutti in a house overlooking the square in front of the station. From the window Gambarutti grinned, held up his thumb in salute, loosed off a few more rounds and then crawled across the floor to join Bellini.

There, under fire, the two men held a council of war. Gambarutti explained that his unit had engaged a force of some two hundred German troops in an indecisive battle which had raged most of that Friday morning. Without reinforcements, he feared he would have to withdraw. Yelling above the noise of battle, Bellini outlined his own situation. A sizeable force of Germans was held up at Dongo, he said. He would have to let them through at least as far as the Ponte del Passo but he would do his best to keep them on the east bank of the lake, and prevent them crossing the bridge.

"Are you sure you can?" Gambarutti yelled. "If they get through, they might just decide to make for this place . . . we'll be annihilated."

"I can try," Bellini shouted back. "I might even be able to blow up the bridge, but at the moment we have no explosive."

"Do whatever you like," Gambarutti said, "but for God's sake don't let your Germans get beyond the Ponte del Passo!"

The two men bade each other farewell as a stream of bullets hit the wall of the house, and Bellini stole away from the battle with Gambarutti's words still ringing through his head.

He drove recklessly back to the Ponte del Passo and issued orders to the partisans there that the bridge must be mined and that they must somehow get explosives. It was there that the ubiquitous police sergeant Buffelli again proved his worth. He disclosed that there was a cache of dynamite in Gravedona and off he went to fetch it. Bellini knew that blowing the bridge would be sensible only as a last resort; what was needed now, before he drove back across the bridge to Dongo with Fallmeyer, was still more evidence of the partisan's strength. The bridge must not only be mined but it should be seen to be mined.

"Dig some holes in the road," he ordered. "About a dozen each side of the bridge. We're going to put mines in the road to impress the tedesci."

"Mines? What mines?" asked Aldo Castelli. "We have no mines."

"We know that," Bellini replied. "But the tedesci don't. If we dig some holes in the road, put some logs in them, fill them over with freshly dug earth and tell them there are mines there, do you think they are going to run over them to prove us liars?"

The audacity of the idea caught the imaginations of the partisans and they set to, digging holes like children making sand castles on the beach. When they had finished, Bellini inspected their work with amused satisfaction for a moment, then called the partisans together and spoke to them in his usual serious tones.

"Remember this is no game," he warned. "There are many Germans on their way. They don't want to fight, but they will if they have to, or if they think they can win. Blow up the bridge if you have to but above all, remember that no German must cross it." With that, he drove back to collect Fallmeyer. He found the German still in the same room at the German barracks, pacing up and down and anxiously looking at his watch. It was just after midday.

"We can now return to Dongo," Bellini told him. "I am authorised to allow German soldiers—and only German soldiers—through the roadblock and permit them to proceed under the escort of partisans. If you or your men make any attempt to resist, the consequences will be grave. Do you understand?"

Fallmeyer nodded curtly. "Yes. But I shall need to discuss the matter when I return to my unit."

"I will give you half an hour," Bellini said. He made sure, through Hofmann, that the German was quite clear about the terms of their conduct through the roadblock, then led the way out to the waiting German car. They drove back to the Ponte del Passo, were conducted through the "mines" by a solemn-faced partisan and then headed slowly for Dongo.

So far, Pier Bellini had won all his battles. But he was on the brink of another—and this one he was to lose.

9

The convoy of Italian and German cars had been stopped outside Musso since shortly after seven that morning. Fallmeyer had been gone with the partisans more than an hour and since then there had been no action, no news, nothing. The waiting, which had thus dragged on for nearly five hours, was an oppressive, demoralising thing and by midday the nerves of many had cracked. While Mussolini continued to sit stolidly in the armoured car at the head of the procession others had decided that surrender would be the best course.

The priest at Musso, a bustling, energetic cleric named Don Mainetti, had witnessed the arrival of the convoy early in the morning, and he had spoken to the German soldiers whose trucks had pulled up outside the church. They had asked him if he would make contact with the partisans so as to speed their departure from Italy. The priest had returned to his church from this mission at about midday, when he suddenly found himself unwitting host to a group of the Fascist hierarchy. The first to arrive and seek sanctuary was, oddly enough, Nichola Bombacci, he who had led the exodus from Milan with cries of undying loyalty to his long-time friend Mussolini. Bombacci now came into the priest's dining room and announced that he wished to surrender, asking the priest to intercede for him. He said he had lost faith in Mussolini when it was found that Il Duce was going to abandon them all and try to escape into Switzerland. This was evidently a view shared by some of the Ministers, for very soon, Don Mainetti was surrounded by them. Paulo Zerbino, the Minister of the Interior; Augusto Liverani, Minister of Communications; Ruggero Romano, Minister of Public Works, and his teenage son; Fernando Mezzasoma, Minister of Popular Culture—they all left the convoy to seek refuge in the church.

But if Don Mainetti was a comfort to some, he was regarded as a menace by at least one other—Kriminalinspektor Otto Kisnatt. Trained to be watchful, and a skilful practitioner of the art, he had noted the arrival of the cleric at the head of the convoy earlier in the morning. Don Mainetti had puffed up on his bicycle and had stopped to speak to some of the SS men deployed along the road between the armoured car and the partisan barricade. Kisnatt saw him pointing in the direction of Dongo and he had walked swiftly over to the group, where Mainetti was offering to negotiate with the partisans to avoid unnecessary fighting. His offer was refused, and he had vanished from the scene for a time.

But a little later, he was back and this time he said his services were needed in Dongo, where the body of a partisan killed in the initial exchange of fire had been taken. He was allowed to pass and pedalled away into Dongo. Kisnatt returned to his car after that, and stood talking to two other SD men, lamenting the fact that Mussolini had been delayed overnight in Menaggio. Had they not waited, they might now be well on their way to Merano.

It was about eleven in the morning when Kisnatt saw Mussolini get out of the crippled armoured car and join a group of Fascist officials who were, inevitably it seemed, arguing hotly amongst themselves. Kisnatt approached. Il Duce appeared perfectly calm at that time. It was as if the inability to make a decision of any kind in the face of the present impasse was a relief to him.

"They want me to leave the armoured car," he said mildly to the SD man. "What am I to do? I don't want to upset them." He smiled. "After all, they are the most faithful of my comrades."

Kisnatt was about to answer when he caught sight of the priest, Don Mainetti, on his way back from Dongo. For an agonising moment, Kisnatt thought the priest had seen and recognised Mussolini, but he continued cycling down the road to Musso without pausing. Nevertheless Kisnatt was disturbed.

"You must return to the armoured car, Duce," he said. "It is better if you are not seen." Mussolini agreed, returned to the vehicle, spoke a few words to those gathered around it, and climbed back in.

Ten minutes later, Kisnatt was called to the immobilised armoured car. Mussolini was seated near the driver, alongside the right-hand door. And next to him was Clara Petacci. This time, Mussolini appeared a little more anxious. He beckoned Kisnatt to him and leaned across to speak softly.

"Listen, Commendore," he began. "This lady has just joined me. She is very dear to me and I would ask you to protect her to the utmost, should things go badly for us."

Clara sat silently staring at the floor, and Kisnatt replied soothingly. "I do not think there is any immediate danger, Duce. The armoured car is the safest place for the lady at present."

"Do you know who the signora is?" Mussolini asked and searched Kisnatt's face eagerly.

Embarrassed for a moment. Kisnatt replied. "It is the lady . . . your closest lady friend."

Mussolini was furious. "Lady friend? What do you mean?" he cried "This lady has given the greatest service to the Fascist state. It is my duty to protect her. Remember that, Commendore."

He dismissed Kisnatt and slammed the door of the armoured car but within half an hour he again sent for him. And now, Kisnatt sensed that the burden of the long, tense wait for further news of Fallmeyer was beginning to have a demoralising effect.

"Things are going badly," Mussolini said gloomily. "I have a terrible feeling that this may be the end." In his distress, he grabbed Kisnatt's hand and again urged him to do everything to protect Petacci. Kisnatt again promised he would and Mussolini nodded quickly and closed the door. It was the first time Kisnatt had ever seen real fear on the other man's plump, baggy face.

The journey from Ponte del Passo to Dongo was painfully slow. Bellini who needed time above all else, seemed to be wasting it at every opportunity. Punctuated by frequent halts, regardless of Fallmeyer's ill-concealed impatience, he conducted the journey at a funereal tempo and arrived in Dongo at one-thirty in the afternoon. Here, Fallmeyer received the final ultimatum. Germans only would be allowed to pass—and then on condition that their vehicles be searched in Dongo itself. They drove to the roadblock where Bellini again reiterated the time limit on acceptance of his terms—half an hour.

Fallmeyer hurried back to the head of the column and was met by Untersturmfuhrer Birzer. Eagerly, the SS officer questioned him. Bellini had done a superb job of brainwashing. Fallmeyer's report was exactly as he would have wished.

"We haven't a hope of getting through unless we agree to their terms," he told Birzer. "The whole road is blocked and they've mined the bridge at the end of the lake."

"What terms?" Birzer asked.

"We will be allowed to go through—Germans only, no Italians. We proceed from here to the next town and there we have to be searched. After that, I think they'll let us continue to Merano."

Birzer heard the news thoughtfully.

"There's nothing else we can do," Fallmeyer prompted. "We'll have to accept. Their leader, the one with the cap and beard, has given me thirty minutes to agree."

"All right, we'll do as they say," Birzer said. "But there is one thing . . ."

"Yes, what is it?"

"I'm going to put him in one of the trucks."

"If you wish."

"It's our only chance. My orders are to prevent him falling into the wrong hands. If we leave him here . . ."

"I understand. Do what you think best. It's your problem."

The two Germans walked back down the line of vehicles to the Luftwaffe lorries. Standing near the leading lorry was a Luftwaffe sergeant, and Birzer spoke to him.

"Sergeant, I require your co-operation."

"Yes, sir,"

"I need a Wehrmacht overcoat, a steel helmet and a soldiers' pay book. Get them for me, and don't say a word to anyone."

"Will mine do? I'll get them." The Luftwaffe NCO opened the door of the truck and brought out the coat and helmet, fished out his pay book from his tunic and handed them to Birzer. He asked no questions. Birzer carried the gear to the armoured car. On the way, he told his driver to bring the Kubelwagen alongside the broken-down armoured car so as to make Mussolini's transit to the Luftwaffe lorry as inconspicuous as possible.

Fallmeyer, meantime, had conveyed the acceptance of the partisan terms to Bellini.

When Mussolini heard Birzer's plan he showed little enthusiasm. He took the coat and helmet and placed them next to him, making no attempt to put them on.

"We have very little time and this is your only chance," said Birzer. "Put them on."

A heated discussion then broke out inside the armoured car in which Barracu and Pavolini joined. Mussolini translated Birzer's plans to them while the SS man waited impatiently at the door. Clara Petacci was weeping.

When Mussolini spoke again, there was a note of almost childish defiance in his voice. "You must get more coats, Commendore. For these people"—he indicated the others in the armoured car—"they must come too."

"With respect, Duce," Birzer replied. "I cannot do that. I can only take you."

"Then I shan't go!" Mussolini answered petulantly. He picked up the coat and threw it over his shoulder into the back of the car and followed it with the steel helmet.

In despair, Birzer tried to argue that his duty was to protect the Duce. He had to carry out his orders and there was only one way in which he could do so. "You must put on the coat, Duce. You must."

Kisnatt by now had joined Birzer at the door of the stationary armoured vehicle, and Mussolini turned to him.

"What do you think if this?" he asked in a voice heavy with sarcasm. "I have been asked to put on a Wehrmacht coat and steel helmet and to try to pass as a German soldier in a German vehicle."

"It is an excellent idea, Duce," Kisnatt assured him.

Mussolini sat sulkily for a few moments. Then, with his hand on his heart said softly: "I don't want to do it. I should be ashamed of ever having to admit that I sneaked through under these circumstances. I'd rather fight my way through."

Both Kisnatt and Birzer insisted that there was no hope of fighting the partisan forces, and urged Mussolini to make up his mind and accept the plan. Already, the Luftwaffe vehicles were ready to move. Mussolini said he would think it over, and minutes later, he called for Birzer.

"There is one thing I must insist on, Commendore. She must come with me." He nodded towards Clara, who now sat on the step nearest the door, still weeping silently. Her head rested in her hands and her body shook as she sobbed.

"I'm sorry, Duce, that is impossible," Birzer said stiffly. "I told you before, I can only take you."

Once more, Mussolini threw the coat aside and further argument broke out inside the armoured car as the minutes ticked by. Two hundred metres away, the partisans were clearing the road-block from the highway. It was now only a matter of minutes before the Germans would start to move forward.

Elena Curti Cucciati watched the events within the car with hypnotic fascination. As the blurr of voices filled the hot, stuffy interior, Mussolini retrieved the coat and helmet and sat dumbly listening to a torrent of conflicting advice. Then suddenly, Clara Petacci began to scream. Vito Casalinuovo, the Colonel who acted as Mussolini's adjutant told her to be quiet, but without effect.

"Go, Duce, go!" Petacci screamed. "Go—save yourself. You must save yourself."

Suddenly Mussolini jumped up. He tore off his militia jacket, pulled the German greatcoat round his shoulders, snatched up the steel helmet and left the car. His abrupt move was so unexpected that it left the others in the car stunned and silent. Even Pavolini the firebrand was, for once, lost for words. The only comment came from one of the young crewmen in the armoured car—Elena Curti Cucciati judged him to be no more than a boy.

"After all we have done . . ."

The young gunner's words seemed to sum up the end. This was the end of hope, the end of everything. Mussolini had virtually walked out on them all.

Without a word, Mussolini allowed himself to be conducted to the Kubelwagen and thence to the Luftwaffe truck. Under Birzer's direction, he climbed over the tailboard and sat on a low bench well down towards the front, a piece of tarpaulin was arranged as a screen between him and the back, while a dozen or so of Fallmeyer's airmen squatted on the benches around him. There was a heavy machine gun on the floor of the truck, facing outwards, but none of the soldiers seemed inclined to go near it. Finally, Birzer walked around to the side of the lorry for a last check, but as he did so, he caught sight of Mussolini's scared eyes, wide open, staring from the space between the planks which formed the side of the truck.

"Hide, Duce," Birzer whispered. "Don't look out."

Those were the last words Fritz Birzer ever spoke to Mussolini.

Nearly an hour had elapsed since Fallmeyer had accepted the partisans terms for continuing the journey, and now he was impatient to move. The motors of the lorries whined into life, while Birzer hurried along the road to rejoin his men and their two vehicles. The confusion was beyond belief. First, Guenther reported that two of the SS men who had been sent as guards into the Italian armoured car were not being allowed out.

Birzer swore. "Get the anti-tank gun out of the truck," he snapped. "Set it up in the road and tell those damned Italians that if they don't stop obstructing me, I'll blow the whole lot to pieces!" Guenther shouted orders to the SS men, who swiftly set the weapon in the road and aimed it at the armoured car. Guenther went forward and banged on the door. It flew open and half a dozen people, including the two SS men leapt out.

135

Then Birzer was startled to see a Fascist officer dressed in a Wehrmacht overcoat and wearing an SS forage cap approaching him.

"Do I look like a German soldier?" the man enquired anxiously.

"Where the hell did you get that?" Birzer demanded. "What do you think you're doing?" Nervously, one of the SS squad admitted that he had received a carton of cigarettes from the Italian in exchange for the coat and cap.

"Well, get it back!" roared Birzer. "And you! Get that uniform off!" With a look of burning hatred, the Italian removed the coat and handed it, with the cap, to the SS private.

"All right," Birzer said, mollified. "Anyway, keep the cigarettes."

Fallmeyer's lorries were beginning to move up the road, when Guenther came running up to Birzer in alarm.

"Herr Untersturmfuhrer!" he cried. "The Petacci woman. She's got into one of the Luftwaffe trucks!" Fury, born of days of worry and lack of sleep, swirled up in Birzer and he rounded on Guenther with a scream of rage.

"Well, get her off, you bloody fool! Do you want us all to be shot?"

Two powerful SS men were detailed for the job and they dragged Petacci, screaming, from the lorry and left her weeping by the side of the road.

At last, the whole German convoy was on the move. The SS truck went first followed by Birzer's Kubelwagen. Then came Kisnatt and the SD, then the Luftwaffe convoy. Mussolini was in the fourth lorry of this line. At the roadblock, armed partisans swung on to the running boards of the leading vehicles and gave instructions for the drivers to proceed slowly into Dongo and pull up at the far end of the town square, where the search would take place.

Mussolini's discarded Militia topcoat lay on the seat in the armoured car after both he and, later, Clara Petacci had left.

Alongside it, forgotten, lay a pistol with his monogram on the butt. But the shock of his sudden departure had been replaced by a new hysteria. As the German trucks filed past, Barracu thrust himself through the hatch on top of the vehicle and loosed off a stream of abuse.

"Cowards!" he roared. "Traitors!" He remained aloft until the last of the vehicles—it was Marcello Petacci's car with its Spanish diplomatic number plate—had passed the spot. Then in anger, or maybe desperation, the will to resist flared up in the men inside the big armoured car. Pavolini, who had by now recovered some of his theatrical flair, shouted out new orders to the crew.

"We'll take to the mountains," he said. "There, we shall resist."

The driver started the motor and attempted to turn the vehicle in the road, despite its flat tyres. The result was a stream of machine gun fire from the partisans. The heavy machine gun on the turret of the car barked back. Elena Curti Cucciati, squatting on the floor, was shaken by the explosion of a hand grenade landing nearby. The armoured car trying to creep away was blasted out of the driver's control, hit the low wall on the lake side of the road, and stopped. In quick succession Pavolini, Barracu, Casalinuovo, Elena Curti Cucciati and several others leapt from the vehicle amid a hail of shots. Barracu fell wounded in the leg. Casalinuovo was captured as he tried to escape. Pavolini attempted to jump into the lake, but was caught by three partisans and, after a struggle during which he was wounded, surrendered. It was a stunning coup for the partisans. With other Ministers who had given themselves up to Don Mainetti and who were guarded by Davide Barbieri, the bag of prisoners already taken by the partisans was sensational. The names of the captives read like a Fascist Who's Who. But the biggest prize of all remained, as yet, undiscovered.

Guiseppe Negri, one-time gunner in the Italian Navy, had joined the men of the 52nd Garibaldi Brigade only the day before, when Bellini had swept into Dongo to receive the surrender of the German garrison. For the remainder of that day and most of the night, he had helped keep guard over the Germans. They were in a house on the lake road, about fifty metres from where the town square opened out. Now, he stood outside the house, on orders from the deputy commander of the Brigade, Urbano Lazzaro, to await the arrival of the German convoy and to assist in the search of vehicles. While he waited, he leaned against an old disused petrol pump. Behind and above him, several of the German prisoners, hearing that a convoy of their fellow countrymen was arriving in the village, hung out of the windows of the house.

Negri watched with interest as the long line of vehicles snaked very slowly down the hill towards Dongo. First came a truckload of soldiers in an old lorry, followed by two jeeps, then another lorry, then a staff car and behind that, a long line of other trucks. When the leading vehicle reached the far side of the square, the whole line came to a halt. The German driver of the truck which had stopped right next to Negri stared out of his cab, expressionless. Negri walked to the back of the lorry and peered in. He saw some German soldiers sitting inside, and pointing directly at him was a heavy machine gun. For a moment Negri was taken aback, then, carefully signalling his intentions, he began to hoist himself on to the tailboard.

At the front of the column, both Birzer and Kisnatt were unable to take their eyes from the lorry in which Mussolini was hiding. The agony of suspense was making Birzer feel physically ill. He knew he could do no more now than go along with fate, and only hope that he had done enough. Kisnatt's attention, however, was momentarily diverted from the lorry to a solitary cyclist who came hurtling down the hill, turned across the town square, jumped from his machine and hurried into the town hall. It was Don Mainetti. Kisnatt never knew whether or not Mainetti had actually spotted Mussolini near the roadblock, but either way it no longer mattered. Guiseppe Negri was only a yard or two from Mussolini. And Il Duce was only a minute or two away from capture.

138

Negri's attention seemed drawn to the far end of the truck the moment he stepped into it. Some sixth sense warned him that something was wrong. Perhaps the Germans sat *too* still, watched him *too* closely while he moved down the body of the truck. But whatever it was, he found himself moving almost automatically but inevitably towards the piece of sacking which masked the fore end of the interior. All eyes watched him pull the sacking slowly away. Behind it was a man, sitting with his head down on his lap and quite motionless. He was wearing a German uniform and had a machine gun across his knees. One of the other men in the truck said something in German and grinned, miming the action of drinking. At that instant the man moved, revealing the side of his face. Negri at first did not recognise him. The face on a million photographs was not exactly the same as this one, but there was a resemblance. It was near enough, anyway, to send Negri tumbling out of the truck to fetch help and the first person he met, as luck would have it, was Urbano Lazzaro, the partisan leader who was supervising the search of another lorry.

"It's him," Negri gasped. "I'm sure it's him in that lorry. Mussolini."

Lazzaro was sceptical. "Nonsense," he said. "It can't be."

"It is. The Germans tried to tell me it was a comrade who had drunk too much. But I got a look at him. It's him!"

Lazzaro dashed to the lorry and there saw the Germans sitting quietly, making no attempt to move. Lazzaro leapt on to the tailboard and made his way forward until he could see the unknown man hunched in the corner.

"Kamerade!" he called in German. The man made no response.

"Excellency!"

Lazzaro pulled back the covering and tapped the man on the shoulder.

"Cavaliere Benito Mussolini."

Slowly, wearily, reluctantly, Mussolini raised his head and nodded.

"Yes, I am Mussolini. I will make no trouble." He took off the steel helmet, unbuttoned the greatcoat and climbed from the lorry. On the road he reached inside his coat, pulled out his militia cap and put it on his head.

This was a movement that startled Birzer, who watched the scene from where he stood at the front of the convoy. Birzer thought Mussolini had pulled a gun and put it to his head. But then he watched him walk down the road, engulfed in a crowd of incredulous people. The last glimpse he caught of the man he had tried so hard to protect was of him walking across the square in Dongo while his jubilant captors kept a respectful distance behind him.

At the moment when Mussolini was captured, Pier Bellini was busy rounding up the prisoners who had fled from the armoured car and it was while he was walking back to Dongo that he heard the news. His first feeling was one of elation. The capture of the very symbol of all he had been fighting against in the long, cold, hard winter was the crown on all his triumphs. Soon he was joined by a dozen partisans all chattering excitedly, each with his own version, his own details of the dramatic capture. They passed the tail end of the German column just as the leading trucks began to move again and the soldiers who had been standing around scampered aboard. In the middle of all the excitement of the moment, Bellini remembered Gambautti at Chiavenna and the partisans who were still dying in the fighting there. He hoped that Aldo Castelli and the other men waiting at Ponte del Passo would prevent the Germans from crossing the bridge.

In the square at Dongo, Bellini was met by his friend Urbano Lazzaro, who was the first to give a coherent account of Mussolini's capture. Lazzaro led him through the throng and into the tall Norman arched doorway of the town hall. Inside, excited voices echoed around the stone-flagged entrance hall as the two men mounted five steps which gave on to the middle of a gloomy corridor. Turning left, Bellini was led into a ground-floor room with windows looking out over the square and the lake beyond. In the room was a long table and some chairs around it.

There sat Benito Mussolini. On the table in front of him was a tumbler half full of water. He was still wearing the uniform of the Fascist militia, but it was unbuttoned and it looked crumpled and baggy.

Standing on the threshold of the room, Bellini's memory flashed back to a day in 1940 when he had last seen the other man. At that time, Pier Bellini had been a student at Florence University. Like all students, he had been conscripted into one of the para-military Fascist organisations, complete with the traditional black-shirted uniform in which they paraded on ceremonial occasions. And that day in 1940 had been one of the greatest dates in the history of Fascism. It was the day of Italy's attack on Greece. Adolf Hitler had come to Florence and Bellini had been in the guard of honour lining the streets of the city as Hitler, the new conqueror of Europe, and Mussolini, his equal partner, drove by to the thunderous applause of the Florentines. They had both looked so resplendent then, like masters of the world, like Caesars. That was four and half years ago. Now, sitting hunched in that chilly room, there was little of the Caesar about Mussolini. He looked scared and dejected and his face was devoid of colour. His heavy, tired eyes flickered ceaselessly around the room.

Bellini spoke first. He asked if Mussolini wanted anything and he replied he had already been given a glass of water. He needed nothing else he said. There was a pause. Someone else asked a question, but Bellini was already turning over in his mind the gigantic problem which faced him. What in the name of God was he to do with this man ? While he pondered the problem, the room began to fill with eager inquisitors, including the Mayor of Dongo, Dr. Guiseppi Rubini, who questioned Mussolini closely about his conduct of affairs in Italy. A string of questions about Italy's entry into the war and the ensuing disasters prompted a lively discussion. Mussolini regained some of his normal confidence in dealing with these political questions for an hour or more. Meanwhile Bellini's dilemma remained unanswered.

He sent a messenger to Como to contact the area resistance committee, telling them of Mussolini's capture and asking for guidance, but it would be some hours before the messenger returned. Meanwhile, the list of other prisoners had grown to embarrassing lengths. Bombacci, Liverani, Romano, Zerbino and Mezzasoma were under guard in Musso. In the town hall at Dongo, the partisans had deposited the two wounded Fascists, Pavolini and Barracu, together with the Lombardy leader Paulo Porta, Mussolini's secretary Gatti, his adjutant Casalinuovo and a crowd of lesser lights, including Elena Curti Cucciati who had been marched there at gunpoint when she tumbled from the stricken armoured car.

The Petacci family were also held in the town hall. Marcello Petacci's claim to be a Spanish diplomat by the name of Don Giovanni Castillo Munoz, travelling with his wife and two children, was treated with only faint suspicion by the partisans who were, in any case, much more concerned with the bigger fish in the collection. None seemed to have guessed Marcello's identity, nor had they bothered to question the woman in the fur coat who had been captured with him. She sat in one of the ground floor rooms in the town hall, talking to no one, unobtrusive and almost unheeded in the surging throng of prisoners and partisans.

And Pier Bellini himself was growing more anxious about the size of the crowds outside in the square. It was increasing by the minute as villagers from surrounding communities flocked into Dongo to test for themselves the truth of the rumours which had swept through the countryside within minutes of Mussolini's capture. Convinced that his capture signified the end of the war and the end of bloodshed, they shouted and sang, toasted each other in a euphoria of goodwill. Soon there arose a demand that they be shown the man upon whose shoulders they had long heaped their misfortunes. The crowd surged forward but at the door of the town hall, two armed partisans from the Luigi Clerici Brigade stolidly barred the way. Bellini had chosen these two reliable regulars and they had strict orders to prevent the mob entering the building. They were to fire their guns in the air if there was any attempt to rush the doors.

Bellini had given the order sadly. Such, he reflected, was the chaos of war.

It took an hour for the German convoy to cover the ten kilometres from Dongo to the Ponte del Passo. Armed partisans stood on the running boards of many of the trucks, waving home-made white flags consisting of handkerchiefs or shirts tied to sticks, and at each town the line of vehicles halted while the partisans—now the heroes of the day—were begged to tell once more the startling events at Dongo. At the bridge, the convoy was met by Aldo Castelli who had assumed command of an assorted army of volunteers and regular partisans, armed with a variety of weapons from modern machine guns to ancient rifles which pre-dated the most elderly of the men.

But there appeared to be enough of them, and they seemed to be well equipped, to impress Otto Kisnatt and Birzer, and when the column was commanded to stop by the partisans it obeyed instantly. Castelli immediately seized on the luckless Fallmeyer, informing him that he would have to make one more journey to partisan headquarters, this time at Colico, on the other side of Lake Como. Here, Castelli said, they would be given further instructions. Fallmeyer could do nothing but agree, and told Birzer with a shrug that there was little alternative anyway.

Now, much of the tension which had been evident at the Dongo roadblock had eased off. The partisans, it seemed to Kisnatt, were no longer a bunch of ferocious peasants, but a friendly band of rather bizarre warriors. Some fetched casks of wine and they shared it with the Germans, who in turn proffered cigarettes. And when Kisnatt took advantage of the break in the journey to burn some official documents, the partisans merely crowded round the fire to warm themselves.

Then it began to rain, and darkness cloaked the gloomy valley, merging in one sombre ambience the grey placid waters of the lake, the dark mountains and heavy sky. Hunched in the passenger seat of the Kubelwagen, Fritz Birzer reflected that the mood of the depressing evening exactly matched his own. He was oppressed by his failure to save Mussolini and contemplated the dire consequences that might ensue if he ever returned to Nazi Germany with that failure on his hands.

Castelli and Hofmann came to the Ponte del Passo shortly before seven in the evening, carrying an order from Leutnant Fallmeyer to his men, that they were to hand over their weapons to the partisans and thereafter do whatever they were told. In carrying out his plan to make the Germans surrender, Aldo Castelli had proved himself a resourceful, if undiplomatic, negotiator. When he had got Fallmeyer in the partisan stronghold on the other side of the lake, he had simply disarmed him and at gunpoint, ordered him to write the surrender document. Just after this he and Hofmann ran—literally—into trouble. They were scurrying along in the old Fiat with Hofmann at the wheel, when they were surprised by a pair of German tanks which had closed in on a crossroads between them and the Ponte del Passo. There was a head-on collision and both men were thrown under the dashboard of the Fiat emerging cut, bruised, dazed and prepared, at the very least, to be taken prisoner. To their amazement, however, a solicitous German tank commander had apologised to them, patched their cuts with a first-aid kit from his tank, and waved them on their way after helping to straighten the crumpled front of their car!

Later when Untersturmfuhrer Birzer read the surrender order, although technically not obliged to obey it, he had no option but to comply. Along with the rest, he told the SS to hand over their weapons. As an odd gesture of courtesy, the partisans allowed Birzer to retain his pistol, but soon a whole armoury of rifles, automatics, sub-machine guns and even an anti-tank gun were piled against the lakeside wall. It was then announced that the Germans would also have to leave their vehicles. Partisans would escort them on foot across the mountains to Switzerland and from

144

there they could make their way home as best they may. It was the final humiliation.

In the pouring rain, the Germans now began to haul their hand baggage from their trucks and cars and it was then that Birzer found himself with a fortune at his feet. Among the luggage being unloaded from the SS truck were the two cases which Kisnatt had put there for safe keeping when asked by the two civilians in Menaggio. Anxious to retrieve only their individual belongings, the SS troopers simply tipped all the cases from the lorry on to the ground by the side of the road. And when one of them hit the wet tarmac only a few feet from Birzer, it split open. Birzer bent to take a closer look at the contents, and what he saw staggered him.

There were masses of jewellery. More wealth than Birzer had ever seen lay on the muddy road almost under his jackboots. For seconds, he stood there, mesmerised, unable to gather his wits. Then, something like fear swept through him.

"Into the lake," he snapped. "Get this lot into the lake. Quickly! And the other one with it. Hurry!"

Obediently, the SS men leapt to his command. It took four of them to lift the trunk and heave it into the water. A moment later the other followed with a dull splash and an untold treasure vanished beneath the leaden waters. They watched, fascinated, as the ripples lapped against the shore before the lake resumed its normal placidity. Sweat trickled down Birzer's spine. He couldn't tell why he had thrown away such staggering riches. He only knew he felt better for having done so.

None of the partisans appeared to have seen this strange episode and soon the wet, dispirited Germans lined up in a straggling column and the trek began. Ahead lay a ridge of mountains; on the other side, neutral Switzerland. And then? Like most of the others, Fritz Birzer couldn't bear to contemplate what the future might hold.

As dusk fell over Dongo, Pier Bellini's anxiety about the milling crowds outside the town hall increased. The mob now filled the square and each new voice added to the clamour demanding that Mussolini be brought out and exhibited to them.

The room where Mussolini was detained was by now hot and smoky. The prisoner was surrounded with an ever-increasing circle of inquisitors, while in and out of the room strode other prisoners, including Paulo Porta, who smoked nervously and incessantly throughout the proceedings. At the window, Pier Bellini stared out across the square, deeply distressed by his new and unwelcome responsibility. He was determined to preserve Mussolini safely until he could hand him over to some higher authority—preferably the post-war Italian government, or to some legal body who would treat the man according to law. To Bellini's mind, it was fundamental that if this event heralded the end of the war in Italy, the new era of peace should begin with due respect to the rule of law. In his heart, however, he felt sure his view was not shared by many in the crowd outside. Already, he had heard ugly cries that Mussolini should be shot or strung up on the spot. On the other hand, he could still not be certain that other German or Italian Fascist forces were not in the area, and he knew that his scattered unit would be no match for a determined rescue operation.

His situation was the more perplexing for the lack of any word from Como or Milan. A messenger had been sent to Como and the local customs police were attempting to contact Milan by telephone. However all direct lines were out of order and it had been left with a telephone operator in Lecco, on the other side of the lake, to do his best to get a message to the Committee of Liberation in Milan.

Bellini's thoughts were interrupted by the arrival of Buffelli, who had come from Ponte del Passo to report that the German convoy had been stopped there and was being disarmed. That, at least, was a relief, but it didn't solve his immediate problem.

"I don't like the look of all this," he said to Buffelli indicating the crowds outside the town hall. "We'll find ourselves with a lynching on our hands if we are not very careful. Or there could be an attempt to rescue Mussolini. I shall not be happy until I have got him out of this place . . . in fact, I'd have been much happier if I'd never seen him at all."

Sergeant Buffelli stroked his chin contemplatively.

"Why not take him and a few of the other prisoners up to Germasino. There's plenty of room in the police barracks. It's isolated and could easily be defended in case of attack."

It was an intelligent idea. Germasino, a tiny hamlet high in the mountain above Dongo, could only be reached by one winding road. A contingent of Buffelli's customs police was stationed there to prevent smuggling across the mountains to and from Switzerland. Technically these men owed loyalty to the Fascist government, but had long since been actively co-operating with the partisans, as indeed had Buffelli himself.

Bellini quickly agreed to Buffelli's plan to organise two cars and a dozen or so regular partisans to carry out the move immediately. This accomplished, Buffelli returned to the town hall. Mussolini and Porta, who had been informed of the scheme, were ready to walk out under the escort of Bellini. Mussolini was shivering with the cold and Buffelli snatched up the Luftwaffe overcoat which Mussolini had discarded, and offered it to him. Mussolini waved it aside angrily. "No, no. To hell with the Germans, I've had enough of them. I never want to see their uniform again!"

The two cars had been drawn up in front of the door, where nine of the 52nd Garibaldi Brigade stood guard. Porta entered the first car with Buffelli, and Mussolini took the seat between them. In front, Bellini sat next to the driver. Half a dozen partisans followed in the second car. Mussolini was unable to conceal his nervousness. He kept asking Buffelli where they were going, peering out into the darkness as the car twisted and turned uphill. The Sergeant gave vague answers. Buffelli kept a loaded pistol in his hand with the safety catch open, and Mussolini eyed it frequently as he fidgeted in his seat. For the sake of saying something, Buffelli remarked that this was the second time Mussolini had been a prisoner. With a sigh, Il Duce agreed and went on to compare his predicament with that of Napoleon. Then they all relapsed into silence until the car drew up at the little barracks in Germasino.

It was bitterly cold in the sparse, stone-built room into which Mussolini and Porta were led, and someone thoughtfully gave Porta a blanket which he put round his shoulders. Mussolini refused a similar offer and strode up and down the floor, uncomplaining, but occasionally stamping his boots on the flagstones in order to bring the circulation back to his feet. Then Pier Bellini left them while he conferred with the garrison police. He demanded that the strictest guard be kept on the prisoners. In mid-evening, when he returned, he found Mussolini still pacing the room while Porta sat disconsolate under the watchful eyes of Sergeant Buffelli. Mussolini asked if he could have a private word with the young partisan leader and drew him aside at the end of the room near a window.

"I have to ask you," Mussolini began, "if you will do me a favour." He spoke in a low voice, anxious, it seemed, that the others should not hear.

"A favour? What kind of favour?" Bellini inquired.

"There is a friend . . . a good friend of mine . . . a lady." Mussolini was clearly embarrassed and he jerked his hands aloft as if trying to snatch the right words from the air. "She is in the Prefecture in Dongo. Perhaps you saw her. She wore a coat . . . a fur coat . . . I wish you to give her a message from me."

Bellini was perplexed. "I'm afraid I don't understand."

"I would like you to give a message to this lady and say that I am safe," Mussolini repeated.

"Perhaps I can do that," Bellini said guardedly. "But who is this lady?"

"A friend."

"But I must know who she is. I am not here to run errands for people."

Mussolini held up a hand and Bellini stopped in mid-sentence. For a moment or two there was silence during which Mussolini looked sadly at the young partisan as though appealing for sympathy and help. Then, in a soft voice, he spoke.

"It is Signora Petacci."

Bellini was startled and intrigued. Like everyone else in Italy, he well knew of the existence of the woman who, for years, had been Mussolini's mistress. Like most other Italians, he had heard the jokes and the stories which had been rife since well before the war. It seemed incredible that this notorious woman should actually be in Dongo.

Mussolini spoke again. "Now that you know who this lady is, I beg you not to tell anyone else. I do not believe you will harm her, but others might."

"I shall tell no one."

"You give me your word."

"I give you my word."

Mussolini bestowed on the other man a brief smile and murmured his thanks before walking away, with head bowed. His concern for Clara Petacci was both pathetic and tragic for in sending her this last message he had unwittingly put a time limit on her life.

Though neither knew it, both of them had little less than twenty hours to live.

10

As soon as Bellini had left the barracks at Germasino to return to Dongo, the men within settled down to pass the night as comfortably as they could. Two of the customs policemen helped to make a fire and another offered Mussolini a chair, which he accepted. He sat at a table, opposite Sergeant Buffelli and his men, while Paulo Porta paced the floor, occasionally leaving the room to smoke a cigarette in the corridor. Gradually the guards began to ply Mussolini with questions and the cross-talk seemed to ease his anxiety. Indeed he quickly regained some of his confidence and with his gift for oratory he held the soldiers spellbound.

He told them of many things. Hitler, he confided, had once threatened to gas the whole of Italy and he described his erstwhile partner as a brute who was quite capable of carrying out such a threat. He regretted that he had not been able to do anything to restrain the Germans while he had been in government at Salo because the SS had practically "shared his bed all the time he was there." Then he spoke of Russia and a journey he once made across that vast land. Asked his opinion of Stalin he said that anyone who could govern Russia had to be a great man. Of the war itself, he declared that the Italian people had wanted the war, and that in 1940 he was always being asked why he was waiting so long to enter it.

Once when the talk got around to the subject of the ill-treatment of partisan prisoners by the Fascist Black Brigade troops, Porta interrupted the conversations to insist that he had never given orders for prisoners to be tortured and had actually secured the release of some of them. Porta remarked that he had never been to Germasino before, and Mussolini commented that the people of the Lake were good, honest, hardworking folk.

Someone asked Mussolini if he would like something to eat, and he was served with goat's meat, vegetables, fruit, cheese and a flask of white wine, which he consumed with satisfaction, talking all the while. Indeed, his spirits seemed to rise as he talked so intimately with his captors and there was a sense of friendliness and camaraderie among the men.

When he had finished eating, Mussolini began to pace the floor again. And Porta asked to be escorted outside in order to smoke a cigarette. Buffelli asked Mussolini if he smoked and he replied that he did occasionally, but that he had already had too many cigarettes that day and it had given him a headache. He continued to chat with the soldiers seemingly free from worry. When the customs men asked if he would write a note to say that he had been well treated, he willingly obliged.

During the evening, Sergeant Buffelli had noticed a shiny black object poking from one of Mussolini's pockets. It looked like the butt of a gun, but he said nothing about it. At 11 p.m. Mussolini accepted the sugestion that he might like to go to sleep. Buffelli had prepared an iron bed with two mattresses and blankets in one of the cells. He escorted him to the door. Mussolini entered the room and walked across to the window. Outside, it was bucketing with heavy rain. As Mussolini was turning out his pockets prior to lying down, Buffelli decided to ask about the "shiny object".

"Excuse me," he said, "but I think perhaps you are armed?"

"No, no," Mussolini replied hurriedly, holding out his handkerchief and a number of other objects. They included a shiny black spectacle case.

"Ah," Buffelli apologised. "I took that for a small revolver."

Mussolini smiled. "You are a true customs man."

Buffelli went to fetch an extra blanket, for which Mussolini thanked him, adding a remark about how well he was being cared for.

"Well, you see, you are not in the hands of common bandits," Buffelli replied. "Sleep well. Goodnight."

"Thank you. Goodnight."

Mussolini pulled the covers over him and Buffelli switched out the light, closed the door and locked it. He stationed one of his men on guard at the door and returned to the office. All was silent except for the continual swish of the rain sweeping down the valley of the lake, driven by a gusty wind which threw handfuls of raindrops spattering against the windows.

Pier Bellini was almost drenched as he ran from his car into the Dongo town hall. He pushed his way through the throng of partisans who stood about in the corridors and began his search for the woman in the fur coat. Without much difficulty he found her in a ground-floor room, still under guard but otherwise ignored. Once in the room, Bellini dismissed the guard and closed the door behind him.

Petacci, looking pale and drawn, sat on a chair with her fur coat around her shoulders, biting her finger nails. She was undoubtedly a good-looking woman, with the kind of looks, Bellini thought, that grew on one. Her eyes large and dark gave no indication that she was afraid, although she watched Bellini carefully as he approached.

"I have a message for you," Bellini began.

"A message?"

"From Mussolini."

Petacci controlled herself well. She made no immediate reply, but with a shrug of studied indifference, said: "Mussolini? But I do not know him."

Bellini sighed. "Look, I know who you are. I know you are Clara Petacci. I have just come from Mussolini and he asked me to tell you that he is well and safe."

"I am not Clara Petacci. I don't know what you are talking

about," she replied sharply but her voice betrayed a hint of fear.

"Don't play games with me, Signora," Bellini countered angrily. "I know very well who you are. I have given my word that I will not tell anyone. You are quite safe with me, but you must stop this stupid pretence!"

Clara raised her eyes slowly, and spoke in her normal husky voice. "Very well."

"Then you are Signora Petacci?"

"Yes. But please, tell me what has happened to Mussolini? Is he truly safe?"

"Yes, he is safe. He is well guarded and will come to no harm."

Clara smiled slightly and thanked the young partisan, who drew up a chair and offered her a light for the cigarette she had taken from her pocket. Bellini explained that he had no intention of harming Mussolini in any way. He wanted only to hand him over to a legal authority who would deal with him in accordance with the law.

"And what about me?" Clara asked.

Bellini said that was a question to which he had no answer. He would have to hand her over too, to be dealt with by the legal authorities. He wondered to himself what possible future there could be for this woman who was more intelligent than she appeared and spoke well. He asked her about her life.

"My life is with him," she said simply. "I know what everyone thinks: that I was with him for his money, his power, his influence . . . but that was not the truth of it. I loved him. I still do. Is that hard to believe?" She shrugged. "Anyway, it is true."

Her sincerity, it seemed to Bellini, was unquestionable and it touched him. But there was nothing more he could say.

"Will you do something for me?" Clara asked.

"If I can."

"Will you take me to him?"

"I think that can be arranged," Bellini replied and he rose to leave. As he walked across the room, Clara spoke again.

"There is just one other thing."

"Yes?" Bellini said, with his hand on the door handle.

"If you do have to shoot him—shoot me too."

Bellini once again was lost for words. This calm request shook him. He opened the door and left the room quickly.

In one of the other rooms which had been cleared of prisoners, he found an old friend waiting for him. Luigi Canali was known to the partisans of the 52nd Garibaldi Brigade—and to other Brigades in and around Como—as "Capitano Neri." Canali was their contact with the chain of command within the resistance movement. His job was to liaise with the men who spent their lives hiding in the hills and who continuously risked their lives harrying the Germans and Italian Fascist troops. It was through Canali that the brigades got their supplies as well as their orders, and he commanded the respect of the partisans not only for his rank but for his bravery in doing a dangerous job so well.

Canali was a dedicated and devout Communist, which Pier Bellini was not. None the less, Bellini held him in high regard, for Canali was capable of seeing another man's view, and was also a man of strict principle. An utterly reliable Communist and a man of reason. The two sides of Canali overlapped. He had recently been released from an Italian prison, where he had been tortured by having cigarettes stubbed on his legs, and when he spotted Bellini, he limped over to him and grabbed him by the arm. He had just travelled from Como with his mistress, a pretty girl of twenty named Giussepina Tuissi, known as "Gianna," who belied her gentle femininity by carrrying a large and fearsome automatic pistol in the belt of her skirt.

Canali told Bellini that he had orders from the Committee of Liberation in Como to bring Mussolini to a house in Brunate, high on a hill overlooking Como, where he could be kept in safety until he was handed over to a higher authority. He suggested to Bellini that they take him immediately south to Como and await further instructions. Bellini promptly agreed, and immediately told Canali about Clara Petacci. He proposed that she be taken along as well. To avoid trouble with other partisan groups, and to avoid having to give explanations, it was decided that Mussolini should be disguised as a wounded partisan and that Petacci be given a document identifying her as a nurse. Gianna would have a similar pass.

Canali, Bellini and Gianna were joined by Urbano Lazzaro and the four discussed how best to transport Mussolini with the greatest possible secrecy. They decided that two cars would be used—Bellini's Fiat and another in which Canali had travelled. Bellini, Canali and Gianna would go to Germasino to fetch Mussolini while Urbano Lazzaro would bring Petacci. They would meet on the bridge of the River Albano which flowed into Lake Como at the north end of Dongo. Then, the cars would travel together to Como, from where both Mussolini and Petacci would be taken up to Brunate and kept under guard.

Apart from the drivers, three other partisans—all reliable—were chosen to accompany them, although Bellini knew only two of them well. These were men named Frangi Lino and Guglielmo Cantoni. The third was Michele Moretti, a seasoned Communist and a tough, dependable fighter.

The plan was completed when Bellini wrote out the pass for Clara Petacci describing her as a nurse taking a wounded man to Como under partisan protection. He signed the pass himself and sealed it with the rubber stamp of the 52nd Garibaldi Brigade.

It was midnight as Bellini stood up and addressed the others.

"We shall leave now. You Bill"—Lazzaro's battle-name—"will bring Petacci to the bridge by half past one. Wait for us there—we shall wait for you if we arrive first. Tell nobody."

Together with Canali and Gianna, Bellini stepped out again into the pouring rain and drove back up the winding road to Germasino, where Sergeant Buffelli still sat in his office and where Mussolini was soundly asleep in his cell. When he heard the car arriving, Buffelli went to the door.

"I've come for Mussolini," Bellini said. Buffelli nodded and walked back through his office to the cell. He unlocked the padlock, opened the door and switched on the light. Mussolini awoke after a moment or two as Buffelli stood by his bed.

Shading his eyes from the bright electric light, Mussolini peered up. "Who's there?" he said.

"Orders have arrived," Buffelli said. "You must get up."

"Ah, I thought so." Mussolini threw back the covers and started to get out of the bed. Buffelli withdrew from the room and waited outside.

In ten minutes, Mussolini appeared, dressed once more in the grey-green uniform of the Fascist militia and a black shirt. His eyes were still puffy with sleep.

Pier Bellini stepped forward. "I shall have to disguise you," he said. "I will wrap bandages around your head so that you will not be recognised when we leave here. Do you understand?"

Mussolini made no reply, but allowed Bellini to bandage him without a word. When he had finished, only Mussolini's eyes and nose were visible beneath the bandages. Throwing a blanket around the prisoner's shoulders Bellini led him towards the door and out into the pouring rain.

It was exactly 1.35 in the morning of Saturday, April 28, 1945.

At that precise time two Colonels in the first-floor room in the Palazzo Brera in Milan were in the midst of heated discussion. They had just come from a meeting between memebers of the Committee of National Liberation and its Communist-controlled offshoot, the Volunteer Freedom Corps to which both Colonels belonged. The subject of the meeting was the news, received in Milan earlier that evening, that Mussolini and a number of other Fascist gerarchi had been caught by partisans in the village of Dongo. Precise details were unknown but on the strength of the report the meeting had taken a major decision and specific orders had been issued to the two Colonels. They had been instructed to take a company of reliable partisans to Dongo, seize Mussolini, bring him back to Milan and execute him.

So sure was the meeting that the order would be carried out, they had prepared a radio message for Allied headquarters at Sienna. The signal read: "The Committee of National Liberation regret not able to hand over Mussolini who, having been tried by Popular Tribunal, has been shot in the same place where fifteen patriots were shot by Fascists."

That place was the Piazzale Loreto.

The execution had been planned with a fine sense of occasion. The location itself would be a clear demonstration that the dictator and his cohorts had received poetic justice. A People's Tribunal would, of course, convict him. That was a mere formality.

In choosing the man to bring Mussolini to retribution the Committee had left little to chance. The senior of the two Colonels, the one who was to lead the expedition, was a determined, ruthless fighter likely to allow nothing and no one to defeat him from his purpose. He was a tall, thin man with a long, lugubrious face, large ears and sallow complexion. His black hair was brushed straight back and a clipped moustache adorned his tight-lipped mouth. His dark eyes glittered when angry and though he had a fiery temper he was capable of being ice-cool in a tense situation.

His name was Walter Audisio.

His companion on that fateful morning was Aldo Lampredi, a former labourer, also a dedicated Communist, who had risen in the resistance hierarchy to the rank of Colonel in the Volunteer Freedom Corps.

As it neared two o'clock, the two men were still considering how best to reach Dongo, taking into account that they might have to pass through territory still controlled by German and Italian Fascist forces. It was agreed they should take an escort of a dozen or so well-armed and reliable men, and travel with a car and an armoured half-track vehicle.

For no apparent reason, Audisio seemed to take no interest in discussing the details of their return journey. Yet there was a reason, but it was locked away in his mind and heart. He alone knew that, if a secret plan which he was hatching could be successfully accomplished, there would be no need to worry about the return journey. It was a grim, ruthless and desperate plan, and fate so played into his hands that he was to accomplish it virtually single-handed.

The old Fiat rattled down the hill from Germasino, gained the main road, turned right and headed towards Dongo. In the back seat, Mussolini sat silent and inscrutable beneath the mask of bandages around his head. When the car stopped, he got out and followed Bellini without a word. The other car was already on the little bridge across the Albano river. Guiding Mussolini towards it, Bellini saw two figures emerge from the car. One of them was Clara Petacci. Half a dozen paces more, and the two lovers met.

They looked incongruous, the former dictator of Italy now swathed in white bandages and his faithful mistress muffled in a big fur coat and a driver's cap pulled over her hair. They stood in the middle of the bridge in the pouring rain while the headlights of two cars picked out their shadowy figures. They did not embrace. Clara merely held out her hand to him in a stiff, formal gesture and addressed him almost shyly by his former title:

"Excellency."

Mussolini was equally overcome. "Signora. What are you doing here?" he asked.

Clara's reply was lost in the howling of the wind. They stood looking at each other, utterly lost for words. Then Bellini touched Mussolini's arm and led him back again to the Fiat. Still without speaking, he climbed into the back seat next to Gianna, who was wearing a Red Cross armband. Bellini sat on his other side. In front were the driver and the other partisan, Michele Moretti.

The second car, it had been agreed, would lead the way to Como. If they encountered other partisan units, Luigi Canali would be able to deal with them. He sat in the back of the car with Clara Petacci and Frangi Lino. In front, next to the driver was Guglielmo Cantoni. The car drew away from the bridge and the other car followed, keeping station at about fifty metres behind.

They passed through Dongo where on the opposite side of the square, the town hall was still alive with movement and light. At Musso, the two cars were stopped and with rain hammering on the roofs, Canali talked to a group of partisans. They were stopped again on the road to Menaggio and once they were fired on. Throughout, the watchful Gianna kept her pistol on her lap and glared fiercely at Mussolini, who remained silent. Occasionally, they saw flares lighting up the black clouds over the southern end of the lake and as they drew nearer to Como, the flares were augmented by flashes in the sky.

In Moltrasio, some ten kilometres short of Como, the leading car stopped. Canali alighted from it motion to Mussolini to staying where he was. He wanted to talk to Bellini about the flashes in the sky. Clearly, there was fighting going on near Como. This was confirmed by a local partisan who told Bellini that the Americans had reached Como and were engaged in battle with the remnants of German and Italian troops in the town. The cars had stopped outside the Hotel Imperiale which faced on to the lake. Bellini and Canali walked together towards the iron railings by the lakeside from where they watched the gunfire. Now and again, could be heard the hollow rattle of small arms fire. Bellini thought it would be dangerous to proceed. They would be caught in the midst of the battle or, worse still, run into enemy units. Canali agreed, and said he knew a place where Mussolini could be hidden safely for a while, at least until the situation in Como quietened down. There was a peasant family, a man and his wife, who had been useful to him once before. They were reliable people, he said, and it would be possible to leave Mussolini and Petacci in their house for the night. The couple, Giacomo de Maria and his wife Lia, lived close to the village of Mezzegra di Giuliano.

So the cars turned round again, and after some twenty minutes, they reached Azzano. From here they turned sharply left and took a narrrow road which rose almost parallel with the main road above the roofs of Azzano. On the right of the road was a high wall of a villa, and further along was a sharp right-hand hair-pin bend at the outskirts of the village of Mezzegra. The road became narrower, and finally the cars had to stop. The drivers remained but the rest of the party got out, Canali leading the way up a steep path between two low walls of stone. Water cascaded down the path, although the rain had now softened and a full moon peeped fleetingly between gaps in the clouds. Mussolini walked slowly, with a blanket wrapped tightly around his bulky frame. Clara Petacci was at his side, and it was she who seemed to give support to the man as he stumbled and splashed up the uneven track.

At the top of the path, Canali motioned the procession to stop. He went forward a few paces where the path opened on to a field, and ahead of him lay the white-painted cottage of the de Marias. Cupping his hands to his mouth, Canali made a series of high-pitched coo-ing sounds—a call-sign he always used when approaching the house. The response was almost immediate. Bellini and the others saw a light moving on the ground floor and soon the door opened and Giacomo de Maria stood in the frame of the door with his wife behind him, holding a lantern.

"Who's there?" de Maria called.

"Capitano Neri," Canali replied, using his battle-name. He advanced and spoke a few words with the couple before beckoning to the others to follow. The room they entered was sparsely furnished with a table, a bench and a few chairs and had a bare stone floor. There was no fire in the grate and a fitful light came from the oil lamp which Lia de Maria hung on a hook.

Helped by Clara Petacci, Mussolini almost staggered in and slumped wearily on to the bench. The sodden blanket hung heavily around his shoulders and he apppeared to take no interest in anyone. Clara began to unwind his bandages and lift the blanket from his shoulders. Canali was speaking to the two de Marias, telling them that the man and the woman were prisoners who would be remaining overnight. He warned them not to talk about them or to answer any questions. Two of the partisans would keep guard over them. De Maria said they could sleep in the house. He sent his wife upstairs to rouse their two sons and tell them to finish the night in the hay loft. When she returned,

Bellini asked to be allowed to see the room where Mussolini and Petacci would sleep, and Lia de Maria led him up the stairs to a small room which opened off the little landing.

At 3.30 in the morning, by the light of a lantern, it seemed a cold and miserable place. There was one large bed, a couple of chairs and a small table. There was an empty fireplace. There was only one door into the room and one window. Bellini unfastened the window catch and took a look outside. The drop to the ground was, he judged, about five metres. The place would do ideally as a temporary prison. Well satisfied, Bellini rejoined Canali downstairs, They told Giacomo de Maria to take good care of his charges and to allow them to sleep without disturbance. Mussolini was sitting on the bench looking utterly exhausted and he let Clara Petacci hold his hand as though he were a child.

Bellini then briefed the two partisans on guard, Frangi Lino and Giuglielmo Cantoni, warning them to keep their vigil ceaselessly throughout the night. Then, with Canali, Gianna and Michele Moretti, he retraced his steps to the waiting cars and drove back to Dongo.

Within the humble house, Giacomo de Maria collected wood, kindled a fire in the hearth and put on a pot of ersatz coffee. Mussolini and Clara Petacci spoke little to each other. Clara shivered with the cold and damp, even though she still wore her fur coat, and when de Maria asked if there was anything he could get them, Clara said something to Mussolini, who looked up for the first time.

"Nothing," he muttered.

"Could I have some coffee?" Clara asked.

"It's not real coffee," de Maria apologised. "But I can heat up some of this substitute."

"It's all the same to me," Clara replied.

A little later, Lia de Maria came in and said the room upstairs was ready if they would like to go up. Mussolini made no response, but Clara shook his hand gently.

"The room is ready. Shall we go up?" She whispered to Mussolini as she coaxed him to his feet and they walked to the stairs behind Signora de Maria. A bare electric light bulb in the bedroom shone starkly against the plain whitewashed walls, on which were a picture of the Madonna and a faded photograph of a soldier in a uniform of a First World War Alpine infantryman.

At a respectful distance the two guards mounted the stairs and stationed themselves on the landing. Clara had gone over to the big bed and touched it timidly. Then she turned to the other woman and asked: "Would it be possible to have another pillow? He is used to two."

When Lia brought the second pillow, Mussolini had removed the rest of the bandage from his head and the woman stared hard at him. She hardly seemed to hear Clara's request to go for a wash, but regaining her wits she said apologetically: "You will have to go downstairs. We are only mountain people." Clara smiled and went downstairs to an outhouse, where Lia fetched some water while one of the guards, his rifle slung over his shoulder, waited outside.

When Clara returned, Mussolini was already in the bed. Lino and Cantoni remained on the landing, and through the slightly open door they watched Clara crouched behind the bed taking off her top clothes. They heard her apparently climb into the bed and there followed the urgent whisper of their voices. The sound of the whispering alarmed the guards and throwing open the door they saw Mussolini sitting up in the bed and Clara under the covers with a sheet pulled up over her.

"Go away, boys," Mussolini pleaded as if speaking to two naughty children. "Don't be tiresome; don't behave like that," he added petulantly. The guards withdrew quietly shutting the door behind them and soon the light went out in the cold, barren bedroom.

Two lovers, who once had sought solace in each other's arms amid the splendours and the opulence of the Palazzo Venezia, now found repose and respite from terror and exhaustion in the squalid bed of a peasant's cottage in the lonely Italian hills above Mezzegra.

It was the last time Mussolini and his adoring mistress would share a bed together.

At four that morning, Walter Audisio watched a driver washing a Fiat 1100 in the courtyard at the Palazzo Brera. It was fresh and cloudy and Audisio thought the rain would not be long in coming. In the distance, he could hear the sound of machine gun fire. He had chosen the Fiat 1100 to take him and Lampredi on the mission they were about to undertake. He had spoken with the regional commander of the Volunteer Freedom Corps about taking a detachment of men with him, and had been told that a crack unit of the partisan force—the Oltre Po Pavesi—was now quartered in a school in the Viale Romagna in Milan. This unit which could provide twelve men under a reliable commander had been alerted and now awaited Audisio's arrival.

He checked the car again, and left it in the courtyard while he went up to the office of General Cadorna, head of the Committee of Liberation, who gave him a pass obtained earlier from the Allied liaison officer attached to partisan headquarters. It was signed by a United States Army intelligence officer attached to the US Fifth Army, who had been one of the first Allied officers to enter Milan. The pass read: *Colonel Valerio (otherwise known as Magnoli Giovanbattista di Cesare) is an Italian officer belonging to the General Command of the Volunteers of Liberty. He is sent on a mission by the National Liberation Committee for North Italy, in Como and its province and must therefore be allowed to circulate freely with his armed escort. E.Q. Daddario, Captain.*

With the pass safely in his pocket, Audisio studied a map of the Como area. He had no further details of Mussolini's arrest but by 5.30 he was ready to leave. He picked up a Sten gun and a clip of ammunition and, together with Lampredi, drove from the Palazzo Brera to the Viale Romagna. On the way, they met partisan patrols flushing out every element of Fascism in the city, as bloody retribution continued unchecked. Periodically, there were shouts and the sound of machine gun fire or just the crack of a single shot.

At the elementary school, a setback awaited Audisio. By a comic error in communications, the detachment he had come to pick up had already left on foot to meet him at the Palazzo Brera, and the half-track armoured car he hoped to take with him had broken down. It was now a little after six, and Audisio, cursing the stupid waste of time, ordered the partisans to commandeer some kind of lorry, no matter at what cost.

Within half an hour, a lorry arrived. A small vehicle, little more than a van, with the name of its owners, the Societa Electrica Ovesticino, painted on the side. Now Audisio waited impatiently for the return of his escort to obey any orders he would give them. They were led by a veteran Communist fighter named Riccardo Mordini, a man who had seen action with the International Brigade in the Spanish Civil War. Audisio gave the escort commander a brief outline of the mission, without divulging the principal object. Immediately afterwards, he, Lampredi and Mordini drove off in the Fiat 1100, followed by the twelve partisans in the van. They headed out of the northern suburbs of Milan on the minor road to Como. As they left the city behind them it began to drizzle.

The little group met only one hold-up on the journey, a partisan roadblock, where they were halted briefly. Apart from this they saw not a soul until the outskirts of Como where, they were told, fighting was still going on in parts of the town, against isolated groups of trapped Germans and a few determined Blackshirt units still holding out. Nevertheless they drove right to the centre of Como without incident and Audisio ordered the car and the van to park in a street near the Prefecture. Here, to Audisio's fury, another hitch occurred. The driver of the van said the vehicle was unfit to go any further. They would need a replacement.

In the Prefecture, the members of the local Committee had been hastily assembled to meet Audisio, but they had not anticipated the furious figure in a raincoat and a silk scarf who now angrily demanded attention. He was met by the new Prefect of Como, a calm and methodical lawyer named Gino Bertinelli, who asked for his credentials. With a gesture of annoyance, Audisio produced his Volunteer Corps pass, a yellow slip of paper identifying him as Colonel Valerio and stamped with the five-pointed red star of the Corps Command. Bertinelli inspected the pass carefully while Audisio waited in agitation. Bertinelli remarked at last that the document was insufficient to allow him to give unqualified co-operation. After all, there were dozens of such passes. Fuming, Audisio thrust the authority signed by Captain Daddario into the Prefect's hand.

"Have you not been informed of our arrival?" Audisio shouted.

"Yes, but we wish to know more about all this. What exactly do you intend doing here?" inquired the Prefect.

As calmly as he could, Audisio explained that he had come to the lake to take charge of Mussolini and the other Fascist leaders who had been held in Dongo. In silence, Bertinelli handed back the pass. It was obvious to Audisio that the men in the Como Prefecture resented his presence. Bertinelli had taken an instant dislike to the arrogant man in the raincoat who, so it seemed, was about to take over and change the plans which had already been made for dealing with Mussolini. The hostility in the Prefectorial office, where Mussolini himself had stayed only three days before, crackled in the air like an electrical charge.

"I am afraid," Bertinelli said coolly, "that arrangements have already been agreed with the command of the 52nd Garibaldi Brigade to transfer the prisoners to Como tomorrow or the day after."

This was too much for Audisio. Trembling with the effort to control his temper, he retorted acidly that talk of tomorrow or the day after tomorrow was tantamount to never.

"I have an order to carry out," he fumed. "An order from an authority superior to your provincial organisation! There are precise reasons why this order must be implemented in the briefest possible time, and I demand your full co-operation."

Understandably, Bertinelli was reluctant to commit himself to the angry Colonel from Milan. Politics in Italy, as the war drew to a close, were confused and factional and rivalries which had been subdued by the urgency of fighting a common enemy were now beginning to fly their individual flags. Fascism was rightly dying from the death-blows being dealt it from all sides but its architects might well have died laughing had they known how stupidly divided were the forces battling for power in war-torn Italy. The scene in the Prefecture in Como that morning was typical of the tension, suspicion and contempt with which each splinter group viewed the other.

When the argument had proceeded for some time without resolve, the Prefect told Audisio that the Committee wished to discuss the situation in private before giving their support. Audisio, together with Lampredi, withdrew to a room where everything seemed to be in disarray. Audisio and Lampredi looked out on to the square courtyard. The rain, which had been falling steadily since they had left Milan, had stopped and the sun shone fitfully through the clouds. The two Colonels paced the room and talked intermittently for nearly an hour before they were called back into the Prefect's office. Audisio noted the time. It was 9.45 a.m.

The Committee informed Audisio they were prepared to give him their co-operation provided he took with him on his mission two of their numbers to act as observers for the Como Committee. The men were the President of the local Committee, Oscar Sforni, and a local Commander, Major Cosimo de Angelis.

Only on this condition, would they be prepared to fall in with Audisio's request for a large lorry and help get him to Dongo. Audisio angrily retorted that the Como Committee was obstructing him, with its talk about permits for the lorry, receipts for the prisoners, prisoners of war, etc. Shouting that he had had enough of this bargaining, he sent Lampredi out to telephone headquarters in Milan. Lampredi went out, leaving Audisio still arguing with a crowd of Como Committee officials. At eleven o'clock his call to Milan came through. Audisio yelled that he wished to take the call alone and ordered the crowd to leave the room. When they refused, he produced his pistol and waved it in the air, threatening to shoot if they persisted. They left.

The call apparently satisfied Audisio that he had the superior authority and, armed with this reassurance, he strode from the room looking for the Committee members. Finding no one, he went into the street and rejoined his escort only to learn that Lampredi and Mordini had decided to act independently, taken his car and driven off towards Dongo. The infuriated Audisio dashed back to the Prefecture and demanded that the Committee provide him immediately with a large covered lorry.

At 11.20, a lorry of sorts was found, but it turned out to be a gas-driven vehicle with fuel enough for only forty kilometres. He would need to drive at least 150 kilometres to get to Dongo and return to Milan.

Audisio exploded. "This is sabotage," he screamed. "You can sabotage whatever you like but not me, do you understand?" Once again he demanded a big, covered lorry sufficient to hold all the prisoners, and he was given yet another vehicle. It was an ambulance, and quite useless for his purposes.

By now it was 11.50. In six hours, he had achieved practically nothing and had lost his two lieutenants. For a less determined man, the expedition might well have ended there in complete disaster, but Audisio was not one to give up easily, despite what he considered the insubordination and treachery of those who were supposed to help him.

He decided to waste no more time and, without further ado, he commandeered two cars parked in the street—a Lancia Aprillia and an Alfa-Romeo Spyder—bundled Sforni and de Angelis into the Aprillia, got into the Alfa and ordered his escort to hang on as best they could. Then, with armed men squeezed on the running boards of both cars, the strange convoy moved through the streets of Como, heading for the lake road.

They had gone about a kilometre when fortune at last smiled on Audisio. Coming towards them on the empty road he spotted a large lorry, exactly the vehicle he needed—a large covered furniture lorry, painted a dull yellow. Audisio's men blocked the middle of the road and stopped the lorry. Audisio told the three occupants that he was commandeering their vehicle in the name of the Committee of Liberation and ordered the driver and his two companions to get out.

"Go to the Prefecture," he advised them. "And tell them your vehicle has been requisitioned. We shall return it to you as soon as we can."

Now, possessed of the vehicle he wanted, Audisio got into the cab and told his driver, a partisan named Barba, to get to Dongo at top speed. Barba complained he had never driven a lorry like that before, but Audisio brushed aside his objections.

"Come on, Barba," he cried, pressing the klaxon horn out of sheer delight. "Let's get to Dongo. I promise you'll be well rewarded if you get there before"— he consulted his pocket watch—"before two o'clock!"

Barba trod on the accelerator and the big truck gathered speed, chasing the Aprillia which had gone on ahead and followed by the rest of the partisan escort in the Alfa-Romeo.

It was already nearly one o'clock. Mussolini's hearse was on its way.

It was about eleven o'clock when Lia de Maria went out to work in the fields at the back of her house in the bright morning sunshine. While working there, she looked back at the house and saw Mussolini and Petacci at the window of their room peering out across the lake to the mountains on the other side.

Mussolini was pointing with his arm towards the mountains, and Petacci was apparently listening to his description of the scene. They were like two tourists enjoying the magnificent view and the warmth of a spring morning. A little later, when Lia went up to the room and knocked on the door, it was opened by one of the young guards. Inside, she saw Mussolini, who unlike the apparently carefree guide she had observed earlier, now looked tired and depressed. His eyes were red as if with lack of sleep and his face was pale. He needed a shave and he sat disconsolately on the bed by the window, making no attempt to speak to anyone. Signora de Maria asked if the couple would like to eat, and her husband, who had joined her, said they could offer only simple food. But Clara waved his apologies aside and said she would like some polenta—a kind of Italian porridge. Turning to Mussolini she invited him to join her in the dish but he murmured that he did not mind what he had.

De Maria carried a box into the room to serve as a table and Lia fussed around, laying out an embroidered tablecloth, two plates, a cup and two glasses. De Maria produced the polenta, some bread and a little home made salami which Mussolini picked at while Clara ate the porridge. They had to bend low over the box as they ate and neither spoke.

The two guards stood on the landing outside, occasionally opening the door to exchange brief words with Clara. When the de Marias had cleared away the improvised table, the guards looked into the room and saw Clara lying on the bed with her eyes closed. Mussolini had resumed his former stance, sitting on the bed staring blankly out of the window. The clouds obscured the sun during the early afternoon and the two guards sat on the floor of the landing fighting the drowsiness which threatened to overcome them. All was silent save for the infrequent murmur of Clara's voice.

The guards yawned wearily: there was nothing for anyone to do but wait.

The furniture lorry raced round the numerous bends on the lake road at impossible speeds, throwing Audisio and the partisans in the back crashing against the sides as Barba, sweating at the wheel, fought to squeeze every ounce of power from the engine.

Audisio sounded the horn continuously as they thundered through the narrow streets of Cernobbio, Moltrasio, Laglio and Brienno, splashing through puddles and sending up a wake of swishing mud. At Argegno, Barba had to brake hard when he found the road blocked by a partisan checkpoint and valuable time was wasted in establishing their identity. Beyond Argegno there was another roadblock and more questions, and a little further on, yet another.

Audisio lost his calm. "Press on, Barba," he cried. "To hell with the roadblocks, we've got to hurry." Still sounding the horn, he urged the driver to keep the speed up and ignore or run down anyone who tried to stop them. Once, when they flashed through a roadblock, scattering a group of men in the roadway, the lorry was pursued by bullets from the outraged partisans. But at Sala Comacino, someone threw flowers at the lorry and through Menaggio to Cremia they were again welcomed with waving flags and shouts of goodwill.

Occasionally, the lorry was forced to stop while the partisans cleared stones and logs from where roadblocks had been sited. At another point, the lorry was racing towards one of the tunnels which led the road through outcrops of rock, when Barba came head on to a vehicle travelling towards them. By a miracle he avoided a crash by swerving but he hit a wall, ripping lumps off the truck and injuring two of the men in the back. Undaunted, they raced on, but coming down a slight hill, Barba lost control of the lorry and it skidded dangerously close to the water's edge before he managed to pull it back on the road, sending showers of stones into the lake.

"Never mind giving us a bath, Barba," Audisio said wryly. "We'll have one when the job's done."

A few minutes after two o'clock they approached Musso, then down the dip into the town, up the rise beyond, round the spur of the Vall'Orba and there, in its shallow bay, lay Dongo. But another barrier lay between Audisio and the town and he had to wait while partisans of the 52nd Garibaldi Brigade removed it. Audisio was trembling with excitement. At long last, he was nearing his rendezvous with destiny.

11

When Audisio's lorry drew up in the town square of Dongo it was exactly ten minutes past two in the afternoon of Saturday, April 28. He did not get the welcome he might have expected, and instead of the respect due to an officer from headquarters in Milan, he was faced with the muzzles of two dozen rifles and machine guns. Some of the Dongo partisans had indeed opened fire on the two cars following the lorry, believing them to contain Fascists. Now there was a deathly stillness in the town as Audisio leapt from the cab of the truck in the middle of the square.

Throwing up his arms, he yelled: "I am from the General Command in Milan. Where is your commander?"

Sergeant Buffelli, with his automatic gun in the crook of his arm, walked across to confront him.

"Where is your commander?" Audisio repeated, but Buffelli merely regarded him with suspicion, keeping a watchful eye on the other men in the truck and two cars.

"I don't think he is here," Buffelli replied at last. "I think he has gone away for a while."

"Then send for him. I have a secret message for him. Tell him to come at once." Buffelli nodded curtly, retreated a few steps, then turned and hurried into the town hall.

Pier Bellini was inside. He did not like the sound of the man who claimed he was a Colonel from the Liberation Committee and at once suspected his motives. He conferred with Luigi Canali and Urbano Lazzaro, who were equally uncertain. At length, Bellini instructed Buffelli to tell the stranger to come into the town hall if he wanted to speak.

Audisio took the message as an affront. "This is insubordination," he screamed. "I have asked you to get your commander. Get him!"

At last, a compromise was reached. Bellini and Audisio met half way—on the threshold of the town hall itself—where they glowered at each other with mutual dislike.

"Colonel Valerio of the General Command," Audisio said.

"Pedro, Commander of the 52nd Garibaldi Brigade," Bellini said.

Both were backed up by their own men and the hostility between the groups was something tangible. They kept their guns at the ready, each waiting to take their cue from their leader.

"You had better come into my office," Bellini said finally. He walked into the town hall, followed by Audisio. On the way through the corridors, Audisio caught sight of Lampredi and Ricardo Mordini, the missing commander of his escort and spoke briefly to them. When they and some others, including Lazzaro, Canali and the partisan Michele Moretti crowded into the room Audisio ordered them all, except Lampredi, to go outside. He had things of a confidential nature to tell the commandant.

Left face to face with Audisio, Bellini felt uneasy. He had no idea who this man really was and was as unwilling as the Como Liberation Committee men had been to comply with the order of a total stranger with vague credentials. He asked Audisio, first, to identify himself properly. Audisio showed the pass issued in Milan. On the face of it, it seemed authentic and this placed the young commander in an unenviable situation. He was still under the command of the men in Milan—after all, the war was still on. Yet he was still unsure of everything except that he disliked and distrusted this arrogant visitor.

The turning point came with the entry into the room of Luigi Canali. He knew the other Colonel, Aldo Lampredi, very well. Lampredi told him the terms of Audisio's mission and now Canali confirmed them to Bellini. There was now little the partisans could do except put themselves at Audisio's disposal.

It was then that Audisio revealed for the first time exactly what he intended to do.

"I have come here," he calmly announced, "to shoot Mussolini and the gerarchi."

There was stunned silence.

Bellini was the first to react. With some heat, he declared it had been arranged with the representatives of the Como Committee that very morning to bring Mussolini to the prison in Como, where he would be handed over to the proper authorities.

Audisio's answer to this was to discredit the Como Committee. He warned that the two men they had sent with him as observers must be treated with suspicion; they might be Fascist agents. Indeed, a radio message had already been broadcast from Milan to this effect, and when Audisio demanded that the two men be detained, Bellini had to agree.

But he was determined not to allow Audisio to shoot the prisoners out of hand. Shooting enemies in battle was one thing, he argued, shooting them in cold blood when they had been taken prisoner was something else, and he, Bellini, would have nothing to do with it. He was prepared, however, to discuss the list of prisoners and to hand over Mussolini at the proper time. Meanwhile, he would call Milan and ask for guidance from the General Command. He tried immediately to telephone Milan, but found communications still interrupted. He left a message with one of the partisans to keep trying the call, and returned to the office of the mayor, where the discussion had taken place.

Audisio now asked for a list of all the prisoners. Bellini, who had spent most of the day since leaving Mussolini, typing out a list of all those detained, fetched out a sheaf of papers containing fifty-one names. Everyone taken from the convoy had been recorded on the list.

Audisio read through it rapidly. Then, taking a pencil from his pocket, he began putting crosses beside some of the names. When he had finished, he threw the papers on the table and looked up at Bellini.

"Those are the men I want," he growled. "Fetch them."

Bellini saw a feint hope of preventing mass bloodshed. He must play for time. He read through the list of prisoners. "These people are in different places," he said. "You will have to wait here while I get them gathered together here."

"And Mussolini? Where is Mussolini?" Audisio demanded.

"Captain Neri can fetch him here," Bellini said cautiously. "He can be here within an hour. Some of the other prisoners are in Musso, others in the customs barracks in Germasino. I'll fetch them here myself if you wish."

Audisio shrugged. "If you like. Why not take my car?"

This sudden reaction made Bellini even more uneasy. Audisio was no longer the angry stranger. He now seemed confident, even relaxed, and he fell in with Bellini's plan all too smoothly. Bellini had little alternative but to go through the motions of co-operation. He counted on two things to prevent Audisio carrying out his execution scheme. One was the telephone call to Milan, which he fervently hoped would bring a little more reason to bear; the other was that Audisio still did not know where Mussolini was. He relied on Canali not to tell.

It was just after three o'clock in the afternoon when Pier Bellini left Dongo. He hurried to the customs police barracks in Germasino, where he collected a handful of the prisoners, among them Barracu, Pavolini and Porta. He speeded up the operation for although he was trying to gain time in rounding up the men who Audisio wanted, he was nevertheless very anxious to get back to Dongo, where he could at least keep an eye on events. At half past three, he returned to the town hall.

But he was too late. Audisio had already gone out to find Mussolini himself. And he had a reliable guide, but it was not Canali. Bellini asked anxiously who had gone with Audisio and was told Aldo Lampredi and Michele Moretti. And it was Moretti, the dedicated Communist, who had helped take Mussolini to the farmhouse near Mezzegra earlier in the day.

So Audisio had all the information he needed within minutes of Bellini leaving the town hall. And at ten minutes past three he hurried out of the building, accompanied by Lampredi and Moretti. On his way out, Moretti had picked up a French MAS 7.65 mm. machine gun which had been taken from one of the captured Fascists. The hunt for Mussolini was on.

So eager was Audisio to be on his way that he did not even stop to fetch his own car; he simply leapt into the nearest vehicle and ordered the driver to take him to Azzano. The driver happened to be a chauffeur by the name of Giovanbattista Geninazza, who had stopped his car in the square at Dongo to join the hundreds of others gaping at the place where the Fascist leaders were being held. It was by the purest chance that he found himself no longer a spectator but an active participant in the drama which was to follow.

Audisio was in a frantic hurry. After telling Geninazza to drive to Azzano, he scrambled into the front passenger seat.

"Drive fast," he commanded. "I must get there to finish a job I have to do. But be careful. No accidents." During the journey, Lampredi and Moretti said nothing, but Audisio stared intently at the road ahead, occasionally reminding Geninazza to be careful. At Azzano, Audisio directed the driver to take the road which turned off to the right and led uphill above the main road. A few hundred metres up the hill, Audisio suddenly turned in his seat and stared past Geninazza and out of the window of the right-hand-drive Fiat. The car was level with the gateway of the Villa Belmonte, which formed a recess of the narrow road, about five metres wide and two paces deep. The iron gates hung between two large square concrete posts and the walls of the villa garden, about waist high, curved inward to the recess. Above the wall there grew thick bushes. The road was quiet and out of sight of the houses below in Azzano. Two hundred metres further uphill, the road turned a sharp right-hand hairpin bend before reaching the village of Mezzegra and so the first houses in that village were hidden by the trees in the garden of the Villa Belmonte. The spot was completely secluded.

The Fiat 1100 drove on past the gateway without stopping, but Audisio needed no second look to decide that this remote recess on the hill in Mezzegra was the ideal site for the execution of Benito Mussolini.

Geninazza parked the car when it had gone as far as it could into the cluster of houses just below the de Maria farmhouse. There was a porch which led on to a tiny square where the women did their washing. Geninazza watched as the three men, led by Moretti, walked into the cobbled yard.

Then, while Lampredi followed Moretti through the yard, Audisio stopped, worked the breech of his sub-machine gun and fired a single shot into the air to check that the weapon was functioning properly. Then he followed the other two.

Audisio told Moretti to go on ahead to the de Maria farm and to warn the two guards, whom he knew, that an officer from Milan had come to take the prisoners away. And while they waited, Audisio had an idea.

"Do you know what I've just thought?" he confided to Lampredi. "I am going to tell him I've come to set him free."

Lampredi had his doubts. "He's not an imbecile," he cautioned. "He won't swallow that."

"You'll see," Audisio said. "He'll believe me."

At that moment, Moretti came back. He had spoken to the guards and all could now go to the house. Audisio walked up the path, entered the cottage and followed one of the guards up the little flight of stairs to the landing. There the guard threw open the door and Audisio stepped into the room. At last he was within striking distance of the man he was soon going to kill.

Mussolini turned his head as the door opened. He was standing between the bed and the window and behind him, in the bed, with the blankets pulled up to her chin, was Clara Petacci. They both stared with mounting fear at Audisio who held his machine gun gripped tightly in his hands.

"I have come to liberate you," Audisio said with forced calmness.

"Really?" answered Mussolini, nervously glancing round the room.

"Yes. Get ready quickly. We have no time to lose," Audisio said.

"Where are we going?"

Audisio side-stepped the question, "Are you armed? Have you a gun?"

"No, I have no weapons," Mussolini replied.

"Then let's go," Audisio said. Mussolini half-turned to the bed and Audisio, who had been oblivious of her presence, now turned on Petacci.

"You first," he ordered.

Clara slipped out of the bed with some embarrassment, although she was almost fully dressed. Audisio waved his gun at her indicating she should leave the room first. She ignored the gesture in a frantic hunt for something under the bedclothes. She glanced swiftly over the table and then searched beneath the sheets again.

"What are you looking for?" Audisio demanded hastily.

"My knickers." It was an utterly pathetic feminine moment—the last in Clara Petacci's life.

"Never mind them," Audisio shouted. "There's no time. Come on."

Clara led the way, followed by Mussolini and Audisio. They walked out of the house in that order, down the path and into the little square. Geninazza saw them and thought how pale and old Mussolini looked. He seemed to walk with difficulty. Petacci, he reflected, was in better shape. They both got into the back of the Fiat 1100, Clara sitting behind the driver with Mussolini on her left. Audisio did not get in, but sat on the right-hand wing of the car, pointing his machine gun at Mussolini.

Before they started, Mussolini asked his captor a question.

"Will they not recognise this?" he asked Audisio, taking off his Militia cap. Then he passed his hand over his large, cropped head saying. "And will they not recognise this?"

"Put the hat on," said Audisio tersely. "Pull it well down over your eyes."

Mussolini complied and sat back, leaning slightly to his right, towards Clara. Audisio nodded to Geninazza, who then started the car and drove slowly and gently down the hill towards Mezzegra. Behind the car, on foot, came the two guards, Lino and Cantoni. The car rounded the hairpin bend at walking pace but picked up a little speed as it straightened out and the tyres started to hiss on the damp road. A hundred metres further on Audisio called to Geninazza to stop and the car came to a halt almost directly opposite the gateway to the Villa Belmonte. Audisio's timing was accurate.

He sprang from the wing of the car and opened the doors. The driver got out first, and stood between the car and the wall. Audisio then called to Michele Moretti to take up a position a little further down the road towards Azzano. At the top of the hill, the two guards appeared round the bend in the road, and there they stopped. The place of execution was now well guarded on all sides.

Geninazza kept his eyes on Mussolini and Petacci still in the back of the car. Then Audisio waved his gun at them.

"Get out," he barked.

For a moment, they hesitated. Mussolini had gone deathly pale and appeared to tremble. There was an agonised look on Petacci's face and her eyes darted about like a frightened bird's.

"Get out," Audisio rasped again and this time Mussolini stumbled from the car. Petacci followed him and both stood in the road, staring at Audisio who pointed his machine gun at them, his finger on the trigger.

"Over there," Audisio said, waving the muzzle of his gun towards the gateway. Without a word, Mussolini walked towards the wall and stood against it, staring at Audisio with a look of disbelief. Clara Petacci went over to stand by his side.

Audisio stood rigid for a moment then suddenly he began to shout something about the war criminal Benito Mussolini . . . a sentence of death . . . justice for the Italian people.

Mussolini appeared not to understand what he was saying, but to Clara it was as though Audisio was reading a death warrant. Terror-stricken, she screamed: "No! You can't. You can't do that!" She was hugging Mussolini's arm looking from him to Audisio in mortal fear.

"Get away from him," Audisio shouted. "Get away, or you'll die too!"

But Clara didn't move, and Audisio pressed the trigger. But no shot came.

Click! The trigger hammer snapped uselessly and Mussolini winced. Audisio's face was running with sweat as desperately he rattled the bolt of the gun, but still it failed to function.

Clara, screaming hysterically, jumped forward to seize the barrel of Audisio's machine gun with both hands, her pretty face contorted in agony.

"You can't!" she shrieked. "You can't kill us like this . . ."

But Audisio was yelling too—to Moretti. "Bring me your gun. Quickly!" Moretti came running and threw him his MAS. Mussolini realised he was about to die and with a dramatic sweep of his arm he pulled back his jacket.

"Shoot me in the chest," he shouted. Those were the last words which Geninazza heard him utter.

The MAS opened up. Clara Petacci was hit with the first bullet and she slipped to the ground without a sound. Mussolini threw up an arm at the last moment and bullets cut through his forearm. Three more pumped into his body as Audisio continued the withering fire. Four more shots echoed down the lonely road, then Mussolini's body slid slowly to the ground his knees buckling under him, ending up in a sitting position. His left shoulder dipped and he slumped on to the wet cobbles in the roadside.

It seemed to the terrified Geninazza, who watched the ghastly scene, that Mussolini was still breathing as he lay on the ground. Then Audisio walked over towards the bodies and fired a single shot into Mussolini's heart. The body gave a convulsive leap, then lay perfectly still.

The smell of cordite hung heavily in the air, and the two corpses touched each other as they sprawled in the wet road.

Nobody spoke. The time was just on ten past four in the afternoon of Saturday, April 28, 1945.

After a little while, Audisio pulled a packet of cigarettes from his pocket and put one in his mouth. He offered one to Geninazza, who, although he did not normally smoke, was glad to take one.

Audisio pointed to the body of Mussolini. "Look at his face," he muttered. "It suits him, doesn't it?" Nobody answered. Geninazza helped Audisio pick up some of the spent shells which littered the road. Then suddenly a woman's face appeared between the shrubs atop the wall of the villa and Audisio yelled at her to go away. She fled. Audisio, saying he would return to Dongo, ordered the two young partisan guards to remain with the bodies until he returned. Then it started to rain again.

Bellini had been pacing the big ground-floor room in the town hall for over an hour. All the prisoners whose names Audisio had ticked were now mustered in the building but there was no sign of the Colonel from Milan. Clearly, Bellini reasoned, Audisio had gone to find Mussolini. As the minutes passed, Bellini became more dejected and depressed. For nine months, he had been living in the mountains, killing enemies, denying himself decent food and shelter—all because he felt the need to help rid the world of tyrants. The whole of Europe had been embroiled in a horrendous war for six years and millions had died because men had forsaken the rule of law. The innocent had been slaughtered without a thought. That war wasn't even over yet, Bellini mused, and already the forces who represented "freedom" were doing exactly the same thing.

It was no surprise to him therefore when Audisio marched into the town hall and triumphantly declared he had killed Mussolini.

"And the woman?" Bellini asked with unfeigned horror.

"I've taken care of her too," Audisio replied briskly. "Now, we must deal with the others. I suggest we form a firing squad from amongst your men. You will be in charge . . . "

Bellini interrupted him angrily. "No! I will not. If you want to shoot them, go ahead and shoot them, but I will have no part of it. I refuse to form a firing squad."

"You will obey my orders!"

"I will not shoot men in cold blood," retorted Bellini. "Killing men in battle is one thing—this is murder."

"You are the commandant of the 52nd Garibaldi Brigade," roared Audisio. "And I am your superior officer. I order you to go into the square and assist with the executions."

Bellini shrugged. It was still war and in war orders must be obeyed. He would go into the square and watch the executions, but he would take no part in them.

The condemned men were lined up in one of the rooms, amid a jostling crowd of excited, angry, confused partisans, some of whom shared Bellini's views on shooting prisoners. Audisio passed down the line asking questions and studying them one by one. They answered briefly, all except one. This was an Italian Air Force Captain, Pietro Salustri, who tried in vain to make Audisio understand that he had nothing to do with Mussolini and was not Il Duce's personal pilot, as it had been alleged. Audisio ignored his protests and passed on down the line.

At the end, he spotted Marcello Petacci, who was still clinging to his story of being a Spanish diplomat. When he saw him, Audisio's eyes narrowed. He walked up to the young, blond-haired man and stared him in the face. Then, with a triumphant cry he announced: "I know who you are! You are Vittorio Mussolini."

Marcello Petacci protested vigorously—and with all the force of truth—that he was not Mussolini's eldest son. He was, he shouted, Don Giovanni Castillo Munoz, travelling with his wife and two sons. He had quite by chance become involved with the convoy stopped by the partisans. It was all a mistake.

Audisio listened patiently, nodding his head each time Petacci made a point. Then, quite without warning, he began to speak—in Spanish. It took Petacci utterly by surprise since he was unable to say more than half a dozen words in that language. While Petacci stood dumb, Audisio called Bellini's second-in-command, Urbano Lazzaro, and ordered him to take the man outside and shoot him. That done, he turned to his prime task, the execution of the remaining Fascist hierarchy.

Suddenly, the mayor of Dongo shouldered his way through the room and presented himself to Audisio. Dr. Giuseppe Rubini, a kindly, liberal man, had been told that Audisio intended to carry out the executions in the town square. He now came, determined to do what he could to stop the barbarous plan.

"Colonel, are you really going to carry out this shooting in the square? In the middle of a crowd of people, of women and children? I beg you, if you must order the executions, go somewhere else."

"These are the orders of my superiors" Audisio replied curtly.

"I don't care about your superiors," the mayor persisted. "I obey my conscience, and I have to consider the interest of the population."

"I suppose the Germans didn't do this kind of thing?" Audisio asked with heavy sarcasm.

"We're Italians, aren't we," Rubini rejoined. "We detest the Nazis and the Fascists for their barbarism, don't we? I forbid this execution. If you ignore me, I shall resign my position and leave it to public opinion to judge."

Audisio shrugged. "All right, if you are too sensitive to come, don't come." Rubini made as if to protest further, but Audisio turned his back on him and continued organising the execution squad. The mayor stood for a little while, shaking his head in sorrow. Then he went back to his home. Later, as the executions were being carried out in the square of his town, he was writing his resignation.

Audisio refused any protest of reason to sway him from his purpose. Neither did the plea of compassion have any more effect. A priest, Father Accursio Farrari, who came from a local monastery on the lake shore, had been hurriedly called to the town hall to perform the last rites for the prisoners. Just before the condemned were led out into the square, the priest, a fifty-six-year-old former Army padre, asked if he could perform his duties before the men left. Audisio agreed.

"I'll go in and speak to each of them," Father Accursio said.

"No, no, no," Audisio countered. "All together. I can allow you three minutes. Only three minutes, then I want them over against the wall."

It was about half-past five in the evening when they filed out and were led by men of Audisio's escort to the low wall by the lake, on the far side of the square from the town hall. They stood at the edge of the road, which ran through the square. On the other side of the wall was a tiny jetty for fishing boats and at the north end of the wall, a urinal.

The crowd had packed the square tightly and the partisans had to force people back to make room for the procession of prisoners. The firing squad was formed up about fifteen paces from the wall, adjacent to the war memorial.

The prisoners were arranged roughly into three groups. First, the Fascist government Ministers and those who held significant offices within the Fascist power-structure. In this group came Alessandro Pavolini, the Secretary of the Fascist Party, once so boastful, now white-faced with the pain of a bullet wound in his leg. There was Fernando Mezzasoma, the highly intelligent Minister of Popular Culture, with his thick glasses and nervous mannerisms. Paulo Zerbino, Minister of the Interior, and Augusto Liverani, Minister of Communications, were both included in this batch of eight men whom Audisio regarded as the most culpable. The other four in the group were Paulo Porta, the chief of the Fascist Party in Lombardy, and Francesco Barracu, Secretary to the Fascist Council. The latter had been wounded when escaping from the armoured car but there was still a dash of defiance left in this veteran Fascist. The last pair to be herded into the execution ground were a Blackshirt named Utimperghe, who had commanded one of the Black Brigades with which Pavolini had hoped to rescue Mussolini, and Colonel Vito Casalinuovo, Mussolini's adjutant.

The second group of doomed men consisted of Nicola Bombacci, Mussolini's faithful old friend; Luigi Gatti, Mussolini's equally faithful secretary; Ruggero Romano, the Minister of

Public Works, who first sought shelter with Don Mainetti in Musso; and Mario Nudi, a lesser politician who held the presidency of the Fascist Agricultural Confederation.

The third group were there merely to make up the number. There were three of them—a journalist, Ernesto Daquanno, director of the official Stefani News Agency, a Fascist certainly but of no consequence: a minor official, Alfredo Coppola, who was President of the Fascist Cultural Institute: and the Air Force Captain, Calistri, who almost certainly found himself in the condemned squad—and probably even in Mussolini's convoy—by pure chance. Calistri was seen to protest his innocence until near the end. Then, he asked for a cigarette, lit it, and gave up.

"All right," he said. "Do what you must." He died gallantly, still smoking, in a brave, nonchalant gesture.

The firing squad was composed of men from Audisio's escort, plus one or two of the partisans from Bellini's command. Most of the others had refused to serve. Bellini himself was in the town square with a number of his men. Aldo Castelli was up on the first floor of the town hall, watching the grisly charade being played out below.

Audisio had insisted that the execution be carried out according to military—if not legal—principles. Riccardo Mordini was appointed commander of the firing squad and Audisio rehearsed him in the correct textbook procedure for bringing the firing squad to order, to aim and to fire. The condemned men had watched this rehearsal. Some had asked to be shot facing their executioners, but Audisio refused, insisting they be shot in the back. Thus, the condemned too had to play their part and to turn about on the word of command from the firing squad commander.

Twice, Mordini left some part of the ritual unsaid and was stopped on the brink of firing by Audisio, who demanded that he begin again. But the third time, the commander got it right, the firing squad got it right, and the fifteen men who stood in a straggling line near the public urinal were mown down. Some gave the Fascist salute moments before the bullets hit them. Barracu, defiant to the last, turned to face his killers, yelling, "Viva Italia."

The executioners loosed off hundreds of rounds of ammunition to kill the fifteen men, and as they stopped firing, the echoes carried up into the hills beyond. The packed crowd stood stock still, and mute.

Then suddenly, a woman screamed from a high window and in the tension of the moment, someone fired a gun. Within seconds, men were firing in all directions, aiming at shadows, as a mass hysteria swept through the squad like a cloudburst.

It was over almost as soon as it had started—leaving two villagers and a partisan slightly wounded.

Then Marcello Petacci was brought into the square, held by the arms by two partisans. At last, he had confessed to Urbano Lazzaro that he was Marcello Petacci.

Since he had been ordered to shoot someone believed to be Vittorio Mussolini, Lazzaro took the chance of giving the man the benefit of a considerable doubt. He led him back to see Audisio. But when Petacci saw the corpses strewn along the roadside, he broke free from his captors and tried to run for it. He was caught within a few steps, but fought madly until again he broke free and this time jumped into the lake and began to swim for his life. Before he had pulled more than a few powerful strokes from the shore, he was riddled with bullets and his body floated to the surface, oozing blood.

He was Audisio's eighteenth and last victim of the day. The time was ten minutes to six in the evening.

With Petacci dead and the shooting over, Audisio worked with ferocious haste to get the bodies of the fifteen men moved from the road into the yellow furniture lorry which had been parked in the far corner of the square. He ran to the lorry, got in, drove it slowly but determinedly through the shifting crowds and then supervised the loading of the bodies inside, a fearsome task carried out by the escort from Milan.

Audisio then commanded Bellini to bring Marcello Petacci's

body from the water and dump it with the rest, but Bellini refused.

"You did it. You fish it out yourself," he retorted. He turned on his heel and walked away, nauseated by what he had seen and the men who had come to Dongo to do it.

Unabashed, Audisio worked on. By half past six, the furniture van was loaded with corpses, arranged in line down one side. The men of the escort climbed into the vehicle, while Audisio found his own Alfa-Romeo. Just after half past six, Audisio left Dongo.

In four and a half hours, he had created a legend, bloody and gruesome, but part of the history of our times.

12

Lino and Cantoni had kept watch over the bodies of Mussolini and Clara Petacci for nearly four hours before Audisio returned. At one point, partisans from Azzano had approached them suspiciously as they waited in the road with two corpses. But when the local people found who they were, they fled.

Audisio's macabre convoy arrived in Azzano at eight o'clock in the evening. Geninazza was told to drive up the hill to the spot where the executions had taken place, and there Audisio ordered him and the two guards to load the bodies into the car. Clara was the first to be picked up. She had been covered with her coat, which was now stained with blood. Mussolini's heavy body was wet from the rain. On the ground where they had lain together, their blood had mingled, but the rain had cleaned the stones and washed away the traces.

Geninazza drove to the bottom of the hill where the yellow lorry was waiting. Without a word, the men from Milan heaved the bodies from the car into the lorry to join the other corpses. Audisio then waved his hand, the lorry started up and followed his car southwards. Geninazza, still standing in the road by his car, noticed that spots of blood had dripped through the floorboards of the lorry and splashed on to the road leaving little dark patches in the mud.

Speed and care were now essential if Audisio was to carry out his plan to the full. His intention had been to bring the bodies of Mussolini and the other gerarchi back to Milan, where they would be displayed in the Piazzale Loreto—the square where fifteen patriots had been shot by Fascists the previous August. But the plan was already in jeopardy. On the way from Dongo to Mezzegra, the lorry had run into the first of the advancing American troops and had been stopped. Before it reached Como, the lorry was again stopped and both it and Audisio's car were searched briefly by American soldiers. In his anxiety, Audisio had told the partisans to sing partisan songs and when he showed his documents, he took care to show the one signed by the American Captain Daddario.

At one roadblock, the pass was scrutinised closely by an American infantryman who handed it back with a brief: "OK, partisans."

"Yes," replied Audisio. It was the only English word he knew.

Through Como the two vehicles trundled, out on to the road south to Milan. Audisio had been on his feet, without rest, for over twenty-four hours and was reeling with fatigue. In the truck, some of the men from the Oltre Po Pavesi Brigade, who formed his escort, dozed with the bodies of the Fascists at their feet.

Mussolini and Petacci sprawled incongruously on the floor. Their last journey together was nearing its end.

On the outskirts of Milan, the two vehicles slowed. There was still firing in the city and some of the streets were blocked. At 10.30, Audisio's car came up against a partisan control post near the vast Pirelli rubber factory complex in the Via Fabio Filzi. Audisio alighted from his car and spoke to the commander of the detachment guarding the road. He asked if he could borrow some men to complete his mission, since his men were worn out and one had been wounded in the wild affray in Dongo. The officer replied that he had none to spare.

Audisio told his men to leave their lorry for a few minutes and take a rest inside the Pirelli building while he telephoned General Headquarters in the Palazzo Brera. But immediately he had finished speaking with his superiors he was greeted on the street by a highly agitated partisan captain, who demanded to know who he was and what he was doing. Audisio replied that he had already shown his pass to the man's colleagues, adding that he was an officer of the General Command, to which he was about to return.

Without warning, the captain grabbed Audisio by the arm, pulled out a pistol and ordered him back inside the Pirelli factory. There, all Audisio's partisans were lined up and held under armed guard. Things became even more ominous when the unknown captain found a list of Fascist officials on a document Audisio was carrying.

"You're Fascists!" the Captain screamed. "Get your hands up. Over by the wall!" To add to the confusion, one of the partisans who had been sent to search the yellow lorry came back and reported its gruesome contents. This merely convinced the nervous captain that Audisio and his men were a Fascist group who had come to recover the bodies of their leaders. Beside himself with rage, the officer lined Audisio and his escort against the wall of the Pirelli building and ordered a platoon of partisans to train their guns on them. For a moment, Audisio thought the man was crazy enough to carry out the execution himself. Instead he took command of the platoon, gesticulating at the line of men at the wall.

"Fire!" he screamed. "They're Fascists!"

Anywhere in Milan during those bloody days such a cry was as good as a death sentence. But, for some reason, the men at the Pirelli factory failed to obey the order and the captain contented himself with keeping Audisio and his men under guard.

The absurd situation was not resolved until after two o'clock in the morning of Sunday, April 29, when an officer from the partisan General Command arrived at the Pirelli works to find out what had happened to Audisio and his men. He identified them, and they were instantly released. Audisio now climbed on to the lorry to ride with Mussolini and the other seventeen corpses on the last lap of the journey.

The lorry jerked and moved off again, deeper into the city.

Rachele Mussolini heard of her husband's death early in the morning, when the news of the massacre at Dongo spread through Italy and the world. She and the children had stayed in the house in Cernobbio since Thursday, without daring to move amid the constant fighting which paralysed the streets of Como and the surrounding area.

"Justice has been done," droned the voice of the radio announcer. Rachele was incensed to hear that Clara Petacci had been shot with her husband, and steadfastly refused to believe it. She thought the woman had been placed alongside Mussolini merely to discredit him still further.

For hours, Rachele sat comforting the children before it dawned on her that this was the end for her, too. She gathered together a few belongings and took the children into Como. There, she gave herself up to the local Committee of Liberation. She was separated from her children and put into a prison cell, lost, lonely and unnoticed.

A hundred kilometres north, Fritz Birzer and Otto Kisnatt walked at the head of a column of men through neutral Switzerland. They had been taken to the border by the partisans and handed over, totally disarmed, to the Swiss border police who had given the Germans the alternative of being interned or of walking through Switzerland and out the other side, into Germany. They elected to take the walk.

They heard of Mussolini's death as they trudged through a peaceful Swiss village. The news plunged Birzer further into despair. While he walked he could only think that every step carried him nearer to a confrontation with an SS firing squad. It was unlikely, he thought, that his superiors would bother to listen to his explanations or understand how hard he had tried to help Mussolini.

They would only know Mussolini was dead. And he, Fritz Birzer, had failed in his mission to protect him.

Between one and three o'clock in the morning of April 29, 1945, Adolf Hitler was married to the faithful Eva Braun in the

Fuhrerbunker beneath the flames of a burning Berlin. They had only thirty-six hours of married life, for they committed suicide the following day. It had been Hitler's obsession that if he fell into the hands of his enemies, he would be put in a cage and exhibited to the public. This was his nightmare and perhaps his determination to avoid that fate was fortified by the news, which filtered into the bunker during the 29th, that Mussolini had been hung by the heels in a Milan square, to be jeered at by a mob gone berserk.

When he heard the news, Hitler made no recorded comment. He had long since abandoned Mussolini, as he was to abandon everything and everyone else in a final sweeping condemnation of his betrayal.

But it no longer mattered. The unequal partnership was dead—the one half literally, the other in all but deed.

At three o'clock in the morning, Mussolini had almost reached the nadir of degradation. The yellow-painted furniture lorry crept down the Viale Padova, heading for the Piazzale Loreto. The headlights reflected dully on the tramlines and wet cobblestones in the road. The lorry reached the end of the street, past the window where Giuseppe Marchi looked sleepily down in curiosity, and entered the Piazzale. It traversed the pitch-black, open square and stopped by the site of a disused petrol station, where the girders of the uncompleted roof jutted out over the road.

Men jumped down wearily from the lorry and began to unload it, dragging black limp objects from the inside, each one following the other with a dull thud on the ground.

The journey was over.

BIBLIOGRAPHY

Bandini, Franco, *Le Ultime Ore de Mussolini* (1961)
Bullock, Alan, *Hitler: A Study in Tyranny* (Odhams, 1952)
Deakin F. W., *The Last Days of Mussolini* (Weidenfeld & Nicolson, 1962)
Hibbert, Christopher, *Benito Mussolini* (Longmans, 1962)
Kirkpatrick, Sir Ivone, *Mussolini, Study of a Demagogue* (Odhams, 1964)
Monelli, Paolo, *Mussolini, An Intimate Life* (Thames and Hudson, 1953)

Articles in the following magazines:
Epoca
Europeo
Neue Illustraete
Oggi
Stern
Tempo

Articles from the following newspapers:
Daily Express
Daily Mail
New York Times
News Chronicle
Times

INDEX